THE TWO DIANAS

Borgo Press Books by ALEXANDRE DUMAS

Anthony
The Barricade at Clichy; or, The Fall of Napoleon
Bathilda
Caligula
The Corsican Brothers (with Eugène Grangé & Xavier de Montépin)
The Count of Monte Cristo, Part One
The Betrayal of Edmond Dantès
The Count of Monte Cristo, Part Two
The Resurrection of Edmond Dantès
The Count of Monte Cristo, Part Three
The Rise of Monte Cristo
The Count of Monte Cristo, Part Four
The Revenge of Monte Cristo
A Fairy Tale (with Adolphe de Leuven and Léon Lhérie)
The Gold Thieves
Kean
The Last of the Three Musketeers (Musketeers #3)
Lorenzino
The Mohican's War
Napoléon Bonaparte
Queen Margot
Richard Darlington (with Prosper Dinaux)
Sylvandire
The Three Musketeers (Musketeers #1)
The Three Musketeers—Twenty Years Later (Musketeers #2)
The Tower of Nesle (with Frédéric Gaillardet)
The Two Dianas (with Paul Meurice)
Urban Grandier and the Devils of Loudon
The Venetian
The Whites and the Blues
The Widow's Husband; and, Porthos in Search of an Outfit
Young Louix XIV
RELATED DRAMAS
The Queen's Necklace, by Pierre Decourcelle
The Seed of the Musketeers, by Paul de Kock & Guénée (Musketeers #5)
The San Felice, by Maurice Drack
The Son of Porthos the Musketeer, by Émile Blavet (Musketeers #4)
A Summer Night's Dream, Adolphe de Leuven & Joseph-Bernard Rosier
The Widow's Husband; and, Porthos in Search of an Outfit
Two Dumasian Comedies, edited by Frank J. Morlock

THE TWO DIANAS; OR, MARTIN GUERRE

A PLAY IN FIVE ACTS

ALEXANDRE DUMAS

& PAUL MEURICE

Translated and Adapted by Frank J. Morlock

THE BORGO PRESS
MMXII

THE TWO DIANAS; OR, MARTIN GUERRE

Copyright © 2006, 2012 by Frank J. Morlock

FIRST BORGO PRESS EDITION

Published by Wildside Press LLC

www.wildsidebooks.com

DEDICATION

*For Robert and Beth Haas
on the occasion of their marriage.
May it be long, happy, and fruitful.*

CONTENTS

CAST OF CHARACTERS	9
ACT I, Scene 1	11
ACT I, Scene 2	57
ACT II, Scene 3	63
ACT II, Scene 4	94
ACT III, Scene 5	127
ACT IV, Scene 6	158
ACT IV, Scene 7	183
ACT V, Scene 8	188
ABOUT THE AUTHOR	203

CAST OF CHARACTERS

Martin Guerre

Henry II, King of France

Gabriel

Arnould de Thil

Pierre Peuquoy

Jean Peuquoy

Jack Tobin

The Constable

Montgomery

Pillemiche

Coligny

Governor of the Chalet

Diana de Poitiers

Diana de France

Macette

Babette

A Page

ACT I
SCENE 1

The Mall at Paris. A promenade—terrace planted with trees, around it a balustrade of stone. To the right, a manor with a large exterior stair case. To the left, near the audience the door of a tavern. The lower level of the promenade joins the street. Two staircases descend from it to the left and rear.

At Rise

Shouts and distant murmurs of a crowd.

VOICES

Long live the King! Long live the Dauphin! Long Live the Queen of Scotland!

CRIER'S VOICE

(in the lower street) Today, huge celebration of the marriage of Milord the Dauphin with Madame, Mary Stuart, the Queen of Scotland. At two o'clock, at Tournelles, a joust and tournament against all assailants by our good Lord Henry II.

Today a huge celebration.

(the Crier's voice is lost in the distance)

PILLEMICHE

(running) Macette! Macette! Macette!

MACETTE

(emerging from the Inn) Pillemiche, what is it? Here it is, eight o'clock and you haven't come and now come to me as if you were making an assault on my inn.

PILLEMICHE

Macette, I've been a bit ill, always my wretched nerves.

MACETTE

You are indeed the most frail soldier.

PILLEMICHE

But I'm not rushing to tell you—Guess what I've just seen?

MACETTE

Who? Ah—would it be Martin Guerre?

PILLEMICHE

Martin Guerre in person! Two steps from the Mall, there at the end of the Rue Saint Antoine.

MACETTE

Martin Guerre back from Italy! But, what, without his young

Lord? See, everything's locked up at the Manor d'Exmes.

PILLEMICHE

Mr. d'Exmes no question will not return except with Mr. de Guerre, but I am sure of having seen Martin Guerre. And yet, I must say, I found him looking—looking unusual! Him so simple and so calm! He strode head held high, brisk, stomach in. He looked like a captain.

MACETTE

Ah! They say these Italians would make a possessed man of a saint. Why Martin Guerre, a captain. You didn't speak to him, Pillemiche?

PILLEMICHE

No, I lost him in the wave of the crowd. But, go, it was really him or the devil has taken his face.

MACETTE

Oh! After a year of absences, I will see him finally; this good, this dear Martin Guerre. But no—actually, I detest him, that ingrate, that rogue.

PILLEMICHE

As for me, I love him as much as you hate him, tavern keeper of my heart.

MACETTE

What! He's coming back and his first visit is not to his friend, his relative—to the one who's engaged her heart to him and to whom he's engaged his faith.

PILLEMICHE

Oh, trust me, Macette, that Martin Guerre has engaged you. I know the man. I didn't go with him here on this last campaign in Italy because I feared the mosquitoes. But I was for whole years by his side in furious wars, and I calculate that he stands before women as he does before bullets—he thinks of something else.

MACETTE

Yes, yes, I don't know what he pretends to have to do, the mystery maker—! Ah, but if he goes back to fighting, not too far this time, I'll accompany him.

PILLEMICHE

As an inn? (laughs)

MACETTE

Eh! Yes—in the supplies—and I won't lose sight of him—

PILLEMICHE

You are terribly serious about him, Macette.

MACETTE

Ah, damn. All the same, he's a proud man, although so sweet. Do you know he's the son of a great lord, and the real brother of the young Vicomte d'Exmes? Brother on the left hand side, it's understood. He's called Martin Guerre with a mane of a farmer, but his mother was a Peuquoy—like me, a beautiful and nice woman—

PILLEMICHE

Like you.

MACETTE

Shut up! As to the father, no one spoke of him. I think that one night he disappeared, and my late father, in my opinion, must have known something about it—but my father was a character of my type, no gossip, not indiscreet and it was useless for me to question him—I never got anything out of him. But you see I've had my reasons to attach myself to Martin Guerre—and if he's been taken from me—Ah! my God.

PILLEMICHE

What's got you?

MACETTE

Perhaps Martin Guerre's been hiding in Paris for several days!

PILLEMICHE

What do you mean?

MACETTE

Last week, relatives of his and mine came to me from Picardy—some Peuquoy, an Uncle and a male cousin, a girl cousin, and a young girl cousin. They came for the celebration of the Dauphin's engagement. At the beginning they talked to me a lot about Martin Guerre and then they no longer spoke to me about him at all. Is that only chance! Eh, hold on, here they are!

PILLEMICHE

Nice faces!

(Enter Pierre, Jean, and Babette.)

JEAN

He hasn't come.

PIERRE

Let's leave without him.

BABETTE

Oh, no, we must wait for him—hush! Macette!

MACETTE

My friends, I present to you a companion in arms of Martin Guerre.

BABETTE

Of Martin Guerre! (low to Jean) Careful!

PIERRE

Oh! A soldier!

MACETTE

Pillemiche, I present to you—

JEAN

(interrupting her) Cousin Jean Peuquoy of Saint Quentin weavers for the last 225 years. From father to son—it's understood—at the Golden Ferry, rue de Filandiers near the moat. My little sister, Babette Peuquoy—my uncle.

PIERRE

Don't present me to this Frenchman.

JEAN

As you wish, now a hand shake, my comrade.

PILLEMICHE

(laughing) Your comrade?

JEAN

Eh! Why, yes, such as you see me, I am standard bearer—in the bourgeois guard force company of the Bow.

PILLEMICHE

And you fire on—sparrows.

JEAN

While waiting comrade, then I fire on enemies.

PILLEMICHE

You—?

JEAN

Me! I just received letters from Saint Quentin, and it seems the Spanish and the English who continue to campaign on our coasts are giving the appearance of wanting to go around our town.

PILLEMICHE

(delighted) The war's starting again.

JEAN

For that reason, I've decided we will leave Paris, soon after the tournament.

MACETTE

You are going to leave again this evening.

JEAN

Our baggage is on the coach. I don't know if it flatters England much that the Peuquoys are English but I know it aggravates the Peuquoys enormously not to be French, right, Uncle?

PIERRE

Oh! Shut up!

JEAN

So, before Jean Peuquoy of Saint Quentin becomes English—I want to lead him as soon as possible home, to break his head at the head of his company.

PIERRE

Ah! He's gay, he is—he's French!

PILLEMICHE

Well—thanks for your news. They smell of powder, which is very salutary to my nerves. You are leaving tonight! I am leaving tomorrow morning. So, till soon, comrade! (he shakes his hand)

JEAN

Ah! You see!

PILLEMICHE

And you uncle! You are also a Peuquoy.

PIERRE

Oh! No, not me.

JEAN

Come on Uncle! You are like a shamed pauper!

PIERRE

Hey, it's cause I am one. I lack what it takes.

(to Pillemiche) You say that I am also a Peuquoy. It's true—we pushed out some not bad branches of Peuquoy, here and there—but Jean is a Peuquoy from Saint Quentin—Macette is a Peuquoy d'Abberville, and as for me, I—I'm a Peuquoy—from Calais.

PILLEMICHE

Yoicks!

PIERRE

I am from Calais and Calais belongs to England—to be English, that's natural for an Englishman—but for a Frenchman, come on! We've been English for 210 years; I was even young in those days! But I've never been able to do anything about it. I bore myself. I'm a foreigner in my town, a foreigner in France. The rest of you soldiers, you must be charitable and believe us, Jean called me a poor man, ashamed, you know now what I'm ashamed about and how I'm poor—and you'll excuse me for going around like this, an old man begging for a country.

PILLEMICHE

(shaking his hand) Ah, if I were only Constable!

PIERRE

(excitedly) Talk to your leaders! I am, just like Jean, of the Bourgeois Guard, and what's more, as I am armorer my situation has made me captain. Well, there are at least two or three of us who still have a French heart. There's Fort Risbank, which is the Key to Calais by sea—we are allowed to guard it, and if you could—

JEAN

Hey, my poor uncle, they let you guard Risbank because the French have no ships. But if the French had ships, Martin Guerre told you again yesterday that—

MACETTE

(approaching excitedly) Martin Guerre!

JEAN

(aside) Oh—now there's a stupid—

PILLEMICHE

(aside) Watch out for explanation! (aloud) I leave you with your family. Mr. de Guise, the general that I love, is not in France, but bah! I am going at least to find the Constable, the general I don't love—and you will see me again and soon—(he leaves)

MACETTE

(furious) So Martin Guerre is in Paris and you've seen him!

JEAN

We haven't met.

MACETTE

You are taking him from me—you who barely know him.

PIERRE

What! Here it is fifteen years I've provided him with arms—and he uses them!

JEAN

He spent two days at our place in Saint Quentin, last year.

MACETTE

Still, you cannot be attached to him the way I am.

BABETTE

Eh! Why indeed is that the case?

PIERRE

A valiant man who will perhaps lead Mr. de Guerre into Calais!

JEAN

A generous relative who renounced in our favor his share of the inheritance of a Peuquoy from Peronne.

MACETTE

By Jove! At my father's death, he actually paid all our debts to preserve my hostel for me.

JEAN

Well—what's the conclusion of all this, Macette? It's simply that Martin Guerre is the king of men.

MACETTE

I don't say no.

BABETTE

He's so sweet, so reserved.

MACETTE

(sighing) He's too much.

JEAN

Soft as a sheep, and at the same time, intrepid like a lion.

PIERRE

You should see how devoted he is to his young lord.

MACETTE

He doesn't know what intoxication is!

BABETTE

He never lets an oath escape.

JEAN

(noise in the street) He's perfection.

MACETTE

What's that noise?

JEAN

One would say a malefactor being brought.

(The crowd invades the terrace at the back.)

PROVOST SERGEANT

(entering with several halberdiers—to the crowd) Come on—Straighten up. (to the men) Don't allow them to get too close!

SERGEANT

Hey! A scamp who says he lives around here! A drunk! A bully! A sort of thief!

(The prisoner appears, head lowered, between two halberdiers).

MME PEUQUOY

Oh, it's Martin Guerre!

MARTIN GUERRE

God! Babette! Macette! My family—

SERGEANT

Ah! You are ashamed, bandit.

MARTIN GUERRE

(to himself, shrugging his shoulders) Oh, my poor goodfellow, if I had no other strings to twist, and not such a grave care in my head, how splendidly would I maul you and your valets.

JEAN

But Sergeant, what has he done?

SERGEANT

Last night, in a dive in La Cité, a rogue drunk with wine and debauchery, served himself with casks of wine, diced with all the money of his dupes, and left destroying the cabaret and beating up the owner.

JEAN

Now, there's a beggar.

SERGEANT

Eh! Why that's him, that beggar there.

JEAN and PIERRE

Him.

MACETTE

The most orderly of men.

BABETTE

The most gentle companion.

SERGEANT

His gentleness is very nice! Three of four of his victims found him this morning and attempted to seize him. He bruised and injured them, and he was on the point of beating the wife of one of them who wanted to call for help.

JEAN

(indignant) Oh, why that man should be hanged.

SERGEANT

What if they tell you he's the gallows bird?

JEAN

Come on! Sergeant, it's someone else.

MARTIN GUERRE

Or I have a double.

SERGEANT

He's been identified by the cabaret owner, by the wife, by all those he cheated and roughed up.

MARTIN GUERRE

(to himself) It's true they seem to have an air of certainty in their business, yet, I am even more certain—

JEAN

But we, too—we recognize him.

MACETTE

It's Martin Guerre!

BABETTE

The Good Martin Guerre.

PIERRE

(to himself) The squire to the Vicomte d'Exmes.

MARTIN GUERRE

Would today be Wednesday the day in which I think that the devil amuses himself annoying me?

SERGEANT

Hum! All this is quite suspicious!

MARTIN GUERRE

I affirm to you, Sergeant, that they have truly slandered me a little, and that I am not a scoundrel.

SERGEANT

Are you quite sure of that? There are four voices for you but six against you. Still, look, is the Vicomte d'Exmes at home?

MARTIN GUERRE

(with anxiety) Ah! Yes, is he back? Has he returned from the Louvre?

JEAN

Not yet.

MARTIN GUERRE

(with an excited vexation) Not yet!

SERGEANT

Oh, if he isn't here to vouch for you—

MARTIN GUERRE

Eh! My dear fellow, the Vicomte d'Exmes at this moment has other things to do than be here to answer your ridiculous questions.

SERGEANT

Oh—that's the way it is! Well, until the arrival of your master, you will be kept in sight.

MARTIN GUERRE

(shrugging his shoulders) At your ease indeed, if your stupidity amuses you!

SERGEANT

(to his men) Watch over this man. You are not to let him go free unless Mr. d'Exmes in person has told if he has really been mistaken for another.

(he leaves)

MARTIN GUERRE

Oh! How I'd rough you up, big loafer, if I were the other one! Yes, but I am taken, nonetheless.

(to Babette) As for me, dear little cousin, I had hoped you would accompany me to the tournament.

MACETTE

(aside) Will you look at the gallant?

BABETTE

Oh, we are going to stay with you, cousin.

MACETTE

(aside) Will you look at the innocent!

MARTIN GUERRE

No, no, I won't stand for it! You mustn't miss this feast. King Henry II is mad about tournaments, and this one will be magnificent. Go without me, my friends. Only don't leave without saying goodbye to me.

PIERRE

Oh, indeed no, for sure! I have yet to speak to you again you know, about Fort Risbank.

JEAN

Till later. Let's go by the Rue Basse, it's the shortest.

MACETTE

Till we meet again, cousin.

(They leave, by the stairway to the left.)

MARTIN GUERRE

Go! Go quickly and leave me with my escort.

MACETTE

And with me.

MARTIN GUERRE

And with you, yes, Macette, and although a bit bothered by my guards.

(The six halberdiers are leaning on their weapons in a semi-circle around Martin Guerre.)

You knew it?

MACETTE

Truly! It was solely up to you to shorten a bit, this is a very long absence.

MARTIN GUERRE

What do you mean?

MACETTE

Hell! Haven't you been in Paris secretly for a week?

MARTIN GUERRE

You know it—

MACETTE

So it's true?

MARTIN GUERRE

Ah! You didn't know it?

MACETTE

Yes, you lie badly, but you are lying, you are deceiving, ah! Unworthy! (she weeps) After the commitments you made to me!

MARTIN GUERRE

Me!

MACETTE

Finally, that I made to you! And what coldness— you hardly looked at me! You haven't even kissed me!

MARTIN GUERRE

Before these gentlemen?

MACETTE

Ah! It's frightful! To hide from a loyal fiancé who's been waiting for you for the last seven years. You're going to tell me again that Jacob waited fourteen years for Rachel—but—

MARTIN GUERRE

But it's probable that Rachel wouldn't have waited so patiently for Jacob. Yes, for a very long while, Macette, you've been so kind as to admit to me that I love you—and it's certain that I—I find you quite comely and that my God—I cannot talk as I am vexed by these spectators!

MACETTE

In the end, answer how it is, why you let yourself be seen by an uncle, a cousin, and specially by that little Babette! When you hid yourself from your legitimate beloved?

MARTIN GUERRE

The duty of your profession, dear friend, is to gossip—to converse with your customers and your tavern is very well frequented. But, meanwhile, for a few days, we needed, Milord and I, a bit of secrecy.

MACETTE

Let's wager it's a question of this famous mystery to which you sacrifice my love and everything else.

MARTIN GUERRE

(grandly) Macette! Macette! Don't speak lightly of the gravest task of my life.

MACETTE

Right! But in that case when will you have terminated this eternal task?

MARTIN GUERRE

Oh—I don't know, that doesn't depend on me; that depends on the Vicomte Gabriel d'Exmes, my dear lord. He's at the Louvre right now—in order to—and I am waiting for him—oh, I am waiting for him with great impatience! He, you see, Macette, he has the very name, the title, the right; he will have power—and me, obscure, unknown, I can do nothing. I am nothing.

MACETTE

Come off it! After all, aren't you his brother, your lord's brother? Isn't your master your student? Wasn't it you who taught him arms, trained him to face danger, who made him what he in the end is?

MARTIN GUERRE

Ah, well, yes, fighting, riding horses, making enterprises, assailing castles, forcing citadels, but it's his instinct, this young man's, it's his pleasure I don't lead him at all, I only follow him.

MACETTE

Oh—yeah! But I'm kept informed by Pillemiche. At the siege of Metz, tell me, did you follow your master, still unbearded everywhere?

MARTIN GUERRE

At Metz? Eh! It was at Metz that he began to attract the attention of great Duke of Guise.

MACETTE

By Jove! Day and night, you were near him at the breach, shielding him with your body.

MARTIN GUERRE

Me—for goodness sake!

MACETTE

You followed him, perhaps, again at the battle of Renty?

MARTIN GUERRE

He took two flags!

MACETTE

From your hand, and so he could take them, you received two wounds.

MARTIN GUERRE

Me? Why no! I don't believe—but it's not true, you hear?

MACETTE

Finally, you still followed him on the campaign to Picardy—?

MARTIN GUERRE

Glorious campaign for Milord in which Mr. de Guise decided to attach him to his illustrious person.

MACETTE

But the day they paid him that honor, they brought you back, half dead on a stretcher.

MARTIN GUERRE

Why will you really shut up? Why, that's an atrocious slander!

MACETTE

As for the war in Italy from which you've returned, here I lack information.

MARTIN GUERRE

Ah! It's there—it's there that Milord did prodigies! Judge! Mr. de Guise chose him to bring back to France the flags captured from the enemy. It's to present them to the King that he went to the Louvre—and what's more, he is bearer of a letter from Mr. de Guise which demands what he requests for himself—money of Mr. de Guise.

Oh, the King won't be able to say no to him. But why doesn't he return? Without doubt, the Constable who is the enemy of Mr. de Guise and ours, must have made every opposition possible. But Milord has earned that reward ten times, a hundred times—so wished for, sought after, brooded over during so many years of patience and valor—

MACETTE

What reward is that?

MARTIN GUERRE

Nothing. A post—a grade.

MACETTE

What grade?

MARTIN GUERRE

Ah! I can say it today, it's the post, actually vacant, of captain of the Guards.

MACETTE

Heavens! And why that post? What particular importance is there in that post?

MARTIN GUERRE

You would be desirous of knowledge, Macette.

MACETTE

Damn! Yes!

MARTIN GUERRE

Well, I promise to tell you when I've told Milord.

MACETTE

What! He doesn't know, he who leads you?

(Gabriel appears at the back.)

MARTIN GUERRE

Ah! That's him! Till later, Macette, till later!

MACETTE

Fine! I understand, but now I've got you, Martin Guerre, and you'll never escape me again!

(She goes into the tavern.)

GABRIEL

(to the Halberdiers) I met your Sergeant. Release my squire. It was a mistake. Go!

(The Halberdiers leave.)

MARTIN GUERRE

Ah, my dear lord! It's you at last! Well! The King? The King?

GABRIEL

I saw him.

MARTIN GUERRE

He read the letter from Mr. de Guise?

GABRIEL

Yes.

MARTIN GUERRE

And our Captaincy of Guards?

GABRIEL

The King grants it to me.

MARTIN GUERRE

He told you.

GABRIEL

I have his word.

MARTIN GUERRE

But the commission?

GABRIEL

It will be given to me after the tournament.

MARTIN GUERRE

Ah! I was hoping you'd bring it with you.

GABRIEL

The promise is worth the parchment.

MARTIN GUERRE

If you trust divine goodness—we've got it—we've got it at last—this first goal.

GABRIEL

But the last? What's the last? To what great and supreme duty have you been preparing me for the last six years?

MARTIN GUERRE

You will know today, immediately, as soon as we get possession of this commission.

GABRIEL

Come on! Not more than an hour of patience! And while waiting, listen, Martin Guerre—for there is other news.

MARTIN GUERRE

Would you like to go inside?

GABRIEL

No, I must watch and wait outside for the passing of—of someone. See, besides, the square and the streets are deserted, the whole of Paris is at Les Tournelles.

MARTIN GUERRE

Even our commission. Why you think that this commission exists that it's already fully signed!

GABRIEL

Ah! Good Martin Guerre, my, friend, my grade, my brother, hero without knowing it, who imprinted courage and honor to me modestly, calmly, like a goodfellow! You are hiding part of my destiny from me, you want to bear it all alone, I don't know what weighty and dangerous secret, but as for me, I have nothing to conceal from you in my soul, and if need be admit to you, my friend, well, it's not only about this commission I'm thinking about, it's not only that—forgive me—that which makes me so emotional and so exciting.

MARTIN GUERRE

(with a nuance of reproach) Ah, what is it then?

GABRIEL

Martin Guerre! Do you know who I found beside the King?

MARTIN GUERRE

Beside the King?

GABRIEL

You haven't forgotten, surely not, the child with dark eyes that old Enguerrand was nursing in the village, while you were raising me in the dungeon.

MARTIN GUERRE

Little Diana?

GABRIEL

Yes, the sweet orphan with no family and no name. Our houses were neighboring, our destinies similar, our souls kin, you know, I called her my sister. When I left Diana, she was still a child—and since then, I've seen her only once in the Benedictine Chapel at Saint Quentin. But I saw her every day in my heart.

MARTIN GUERRE

And, each day, or almost, you spoke to me and spoke again of this early childhood friendship—which resembles love quite a bit.

GABRIEL

Ah! Which resemble it completely. Also, how my heart beat, when this morning at the Louvre, at the King's left, I saw her again.

MARTIN GUERRE

Who? She can't be Diana!

GABRIEL

It is Diana! It's my little Diana! Today Diana of France, the Countess d'Angoulême!

MARTIN GUERRE

Why whose child is she?

GABRIEL

She is the recognized and legitimated daughter of a noble Piedmontese lady and King Henry II.

MARTIN GUERRE

Daughter of the King.

GABRIEL

Well, what's wrong with you?

MARTIN GUERRE

Nothing, Milord, nothing. And you were, no question, overjoyed at this marvelous meeting.

GABRIEL

Yes, at first. Listen Carefully! I saw Diana again. But after the

King's reception, I was able in the confusion of the procession to approach Diana and to exchange with her some moving words. Ah! The dear soul! She was thinking of me like I was thinking of her—only—

MARTIN GUERRE

Only—?

GABRIEL

Martin Guerre, the day in which you placed my first sword in my hand, you told me I had several enemies but that you could only name one and that was—

MARTIN GUERRE

That was the Constable.

GABRIEL

Well, divine a little why the King recalled his daughter, Diana of France, from the convent. It's because Diana de Poitiers, his all-powerful Mistress, has destined in marriage to François de Montmorency, son of the Constable.

MARTIN GUERRE

So Diana de Poitiers and the Constable are against you without knowing you! And Diana de France—what's she say?

GABRIEL

Diana thought me dead, even so she had not consented. But this very day, emerging from the cathedral, she's going to speak to the king, the generous girl! She will leave Les Tournelles before the end of the tournament, she will have her letter taken the way least encumbered from Mail and I, on her passage—Ah! But look there, her pages—her coat of arms, it's she. (running to Diana de France) Madame!

(Enter two pages, a lady of honor, a squire and Diana de France.)

DIANA de FRANCE

Unnecessary for you to come to meet me, Mr. d'Exmes, it's I who am openly coming to you with permission—almost on behalf of the King.

GABRIEL

What, Madame?

DIANA de FRANCE

I've spoken to the King, my father, as I had promised you—I spoke to him in the presence of Madame Diana de Poitiers and the Constable. The King insists on engaging, and the Constable doesn't consent to release the King. My father indicated to me that, a month from now, I shall be the wife of Duke François or I will return to the Benedictines.

GABRIEL

God! And what are you going to do?

DIANA de FRANCE

Ah! I'm not going to marry the Duke, don't worry.

GABRIEL

Dear Diana!

MARTIN GUERRE

O charming and valiant heart!

DIANA de FRANCE

You, give me your hand, friend Martin Guerre—I remember that you often repeated to Gabriel: "Courage! You must have courage!" Yes, it's very true, he needs it, and a lot! Say that to him again.

GABRIEL

Oh! But there's no longer a way to keep hope.

DIANA de FRANCE

There's always a way to do one's duty. Gabriel, I told the King what you were to me in my childhood, and His Majesty granted me the kindness of delivering to you with my hands the reward of your services in these last wars.

MARTIN GUERRE

Ah! And it's—

DIANA de FRANCE

This Commission of Captain of Guards.

MARTIN GUERRE

(grabbing the Commission) At last! At last! At last!

GABRIEL

My adored Diana!

DIANA de FRANCE

Gabriel! You will have to thank the King again—but I beg you, don't say anymore to me. Don't speak to me, don't accompany me. Goodbye.

(She leaves with her suite.)

GABRIEL

Oh! She's lost to me! To die! To die!

MARTIN GUERRE

Child, be silent! Have you at least the courage of a woman? Do you know if the misfortune that strikes you is not good?—isn't it necessary to devote yourself completely to the duty God has imposed on you?

GABRIEL

Ah! Is this duty dangerous? Is it going to absorb my soul, expose my life? In that case, the moment is well chosen—reveal it to me, reveal it to me right away.

MARTIN GUERRE

Right away? You want it? Well, yes, you are right, right away, and on the spot where we are. Ah—there is a Providence. It's the daughter of Henry II who herself delivers to you this commission of Captain of Guards, and who delivers it to you here, under these trees, touching this bench that's here.

GABRIEL

What do you mean?

MARTIN GUERRE

I mean that near this bench, under these trees, on this square—I spoke to your father for the last time.

GABRIEL

To "our" father, friend!

MARTIN GUERRE

To our father, yes, my Gabriel. It was eighteen years ago. They sounded the curfew. Milord had just come down these steps all atremble, all threatening, as when one goes to some danger, so some mortal struggle. He had got to where you are now. He turned and saw me behind him—

"What are you doing"? he asked me, "Am I not to accompany you, Milord?" "No, I am going alone." "Ah, my beloved Master, I beg you." "What? What do you want?" "I would like to go die with you!" "Child! I forbid you to follow me. I want you to live to watch over my son, over your brother, I bind you to each other. Hug me, and remember!"

He pressed me to his breast. I think I still feel the pressure of his hand, the beating of his heart. And then he distanced himself. He's never come back.

GABRIEL

My father, ah, it's his memory, isn't it? It's his honor which is at the bottom of the mission I must accomplish. Come on! Speak. The hour has come, this commission that you wanted is in our hands.

"Once you have it," you said, "you will be able to act, to choose, to act openly and even to know and resume the name of your ancestors, this illustrious name that I'm hiding from all, and from yourself—like a shame."

Well, I'm listening to you—speak—what do I have to do? Look, I have to avenge my father, right?

MARTIN GUERRE

You must do more than avenge him, Gabriel?

GABRIEL

What do you mean?

MARTIN GUERRE

You must deliver him.

GABRIEL

What are you saying? My father! Then he's not dead?

MARTIN GUERRE

My God! I don't know—perhaps he's alive. Oh, yes he must be alive, I believe so. Come on! He's alive. I feel it, I know it, I am sure he's alive.

GABRIEL

Ah! Thanks! Find him! Free him! Direct me where must we go? When will we begin?

MARTIN GUERRE

Well! Why this evening, right now. Take this commission, Milord, go in to change clothes with the insignia of your new rank—it's been long enough I've had them ready for you—and then, I will tell you what you have to do.

GABRIEL

(heading toward the hotel with Martin Guerre) And as for me, I will follow you. I will obey you—more docilely than ever, my dear elder brother, my dear guide!

MARTIN GUERRE

(hugging him) Ah! You are going to see, my Gabriel. Now that you know that Father is alive, you will feel yourself more my brother.

(They enter into the hotel at the right. After a moment the Constable enters by way of the stairway at the back.)

CONSTABLE

What! It's over here?

PILLEMICHE

Yes, Milord Constable—and there's the hotel of the Vicomte d'Exmes.

CONSTABLE

Eh! Why, this was once the lodging of the Count de Montgomery.

PILLEMICHE

Of that, Milord, I am unaware.

CONSTABLE

That suffices. I am leaving tomorrow to place myself at the head of the army. Hold yourself ready. Go.

(Pillemiche bows and enters the Tavern.)

CONSTABLE

(calling at the back) Hey there! Arnould de Thil!

ARNOULD

(entering wrapped in his cape) Talley ho! Talley ho! Sir, what a fine tracker I am, Milord, I already smell the track, and (pointing to the Hotel d'Exmes) There's the lair.

CONSTABLE

Oh—you aren't meant to prowl in the provinces, my lad! Tonight, from your arrival, you were thrown into I don't know what scandal.

ARNOULD

Oh! I am innocent, since they arrested another in my place.

CONSTABLE

Come on! Listen to me. The Count d'Exmes, who dwells here, has fallen in with Madame Diana de France.

ARNOULD

The fiancée of your son! The idiot!

CONSTABLE

The Vicomte d'Exmes got himself named the Captain of the King's guard, today.

ARNOULD

At the behest of Mr. de Guise! The impertinent!

CONSTABLE

Finally, Mr. d'Exmes dwells in this old hotel of the Count de Montgomery. For these reasons, he is three-times suspect.

ARNOULD

And while the Constable will go on campaign, my diplomatic mission will be to watch Mr. d'Exmes thrive. How many times will I be paid?

CONSTABLE

I will pay you ten times, I will pay you 2,000 pounds.

ARNOULD

Now you're singing a song I love.

CONSTABLE

Only—

ARNOULD

Yikes! Now there's an only which spoils my style.

CONSTABLE

Only I won't pay you until my return and on the work being completed. Without this useful precaution, I know you, rogue.

ARNOULD

Alas.

CONSTABLE

You would go waste your observations and my crowns in low dives.

ARNOULD

Fie, has Milord ever seen me?

CONSTABLE

So—2,000 pounds cash—afterwards.

ARNOULD

Why, before that I will die of hunger.

CONSTABLE

Look, you will have a crown a day, for nourishment.

ARNOULD

Oh—for my empty stomach!

CONSTABLE

Enough, I've spoken—you've understood me. You must be able, on my return to inform me very exactly about this. Mr. d'Exmes, his past, his present, and all he's done in my absence. As of this evening, post yourself there. Good watch and good luck.

(He leaves.)

ARNOULD

(alone, falling seated on a bench, head in his hands) The devil! What's he expect me to do with one crown per day? Two thousand pounds I don't know when, but to begin a night watch, worries, dangers! And for the whole thing, a wretched crown. Ah, how petty the great are.

PILLEMICHE

(heaving the run) Ah! It's you! Hello, or rather, good evening, Martin Guerre.

ARNOULD

(between his teeth) What's he saying?

PILLEMICHE

They sent me to see if you'd returned. I'm going to tell them you are here.

(He goes back into the inn.)

ARNOULD

They take me for Martin Guerre. Will I be compromised?

(Pierre, Jean and Babette emerge from Inn.)

JEAN

Ah! There he is! We were looking for you, Martin Guerre.

ARNOULD

(to himself) Martin Guerre again!

PIERRE

We were looking for you to say goodbye.

BABETTE

Sadly, it's the time of opportunity.

(Arnould imposes silence on them by means of mysterious and uneasy gestures.)

JEAN

What's the matter with you? Ah! Mr. d'Exmes? You are expecting him?

BABETTE

Yes, your grand business.

PIERRE

We will leave you. But don't forget Fort Risbank.

BABETTE

Goodbye, my cousin.

ARNOULD

Hush.

(He embraces her.)

BABETTE

The way you kiss me. Ah! Yes, it's for goodbye. Well, goodbye—you will write us, say so—

PIERRE and JEAN

Goodbye! Goodbye!

(Arnould increases his gestures to Pierre and Jean and his kisses to Babette, silently leading them to the stairway at the back.)

(They leave.)

ARNOULD

Hush!

(He kisses her, points her to the Hotel d'Exmes, and escorts her to the doorway of the tavern.)

MACETTE

What? What do you mean? Mr. d'Exmes? He's going to come.

(Arnould kisses her.)

MACETTE

What's this? How sweet you are tonight! Ah, you want me to leave you?

(She remains for a moment in the door of the inn.)

ARNOULD

(to himself) It seems there's a Martin Guerre that I resemble—and he belongs to Mr. d'Exmes. Oh, if I could see him leave.

(He stations himself behind a large tree.)

MACETTE

(to herself) What's wrong with him, really? Always, his mystery. But how sweet he was tonight.

(She goes in.)

(Gabriel and Martin emerge from the hotel.)

GABRIEL

And now, Martin Guerre, where are we going?

MARTIN GUERRE

We are going to the Louvre, to the Guard Room. You are going to make an inspection as of this evening. And as of tomorrow, you will enter your function through the most important and most precious duty in your charge.

GABRIEL

Which is?

MARTIN GUERRE

The inspection of prisons and forts in Paris.

CURTAIN

ACT I
SCENE 2

The underground of the chalet. To the right, the top of a staircase occupies a third of the elevated stage. On this landing to the right, a door near the audience, the first step of a superior staircase, to the left at the back, the beginning of a corridor. A dungeon—cell at an angle occupies the right side of the stage. In this cell, near a pillar, a prisoner, bearded with white hair, seated on a stone and turned towards the wall—hiding his head in his hands.

At rise, Gabriel, Martin Guerre, the Governor of the Chalet and a turn-key carrying a torch enter onto the landing by the door at the right.

GOVERNOR

The prisoner you just saw is the last, Captain of the Guard. Since you've finished your inspection of the Bastilles of Paris with the Chalet, I hope you haven't found anything in less good order than the other prisons.

GABRIEL

There's nothing to be answerable for, Milord Governor. But have we actually seen all the cells?

GOVERNOR

Yes, the usual inspection is complete and you can, sir, return to daylight.

MARTIN GUERRE

Pardon, Governor, I see yet another mention in the register that you gave me to hold.

(reading) X—prisoner secret—"if in the inspection of a governor or captain of the guards he merely tried to speak, have taken into a deeper and harsher cell."

GABRIEL

Who is this prisoner that's so important? Can one know?

GOVERNOR

No one knows. I received the prisoner from my predecessor as he had received him from his. His captivity must go back to the reign of Frances I. You see that on the register of incarceration the date of his entry is in blank.

MARTIN GUERRE

I read only this notation: Cell XIII, Cell XVI.

GOVERNOR

The unlucky man, despite the prohibition tried twice to speak. But at the first word, the governor under the most severe penalties, locked the gate of his prison and had him taken to a stricter prison. That was done twice. There remains only one more terrible cell in the Chalet than his and that airless cell would kill him. Perhaps he wanted it to come to that. But for many years, the prisoner has been silent.

GABRIEL

My God!

GOVERNOR

The man buried alive like this must be some formidable criminal. He remains constantly enchained, and his jailor, worried even of the possibility of an escape, enters his cell at every hour.

GABRIEL

(low to Martin Guerre) Oh! Friend.

MARTIN GUERRE

(low) Courage! You must have courage.

GABRIEL

(aloud) Isn't it my duty, sir, to verify the presence of the prisoner.

GOVERNOR

In that case, Captain, you will take care to entirely omit this visit in your report, and to render an account only verbally.

GABRIEL

To whom.

GOVERNOR

To the Constable, and to him alone.

MARTIN GUERRE

(aside) To the Constable!

GABRIEL

That suffices. Let's descend to this cell—through this tomb.

GOVERNOR

Sir, from pity, don't provoke in any way the prisoner to speak. I repeat that to transfer him into a worse cell than his would be the equivalent of killing him.

GABRIEL

Come on.

(They disappear into the corridor. The turn-keys open the door at the left, always holding torches—going down into the first cell followed by the Governor and Martin Guerre.)

GOVERNOR

Where is the prisoner? Ah—there he is.

(The prisoner emerges from the shadow of the pillar, rises, places his hand in front of his eyes, as if blinded, by the gleam of the torch! Then, rests his glance on Gabriel, then Martin Guerre. He falls back in his seat indifferently.)

GABRIEL

(turning toward Martin Guerre) Ah! Martin Guerre.

(At this name, the prisoner shivers, rises, and utters a shout at Martin Guerre, who takes the torch from the hands of the turnkey to light his face, the prisoner, bewildered, opens his mouth and is going to scream.)

GABRIEL

(with shock) Don't speak.

(The prisoner, as if terrified of himself, places his fists before his mouth to prevent himself from speaking.)

MARTIN GUERRE

No—don't speak, Milord; as for myself, I can speak, I will speak, don't worry.

GOVERNOR

Oh! If you know something of the secret enshrouded in this cell, remember you mustn't say anything, except to the Constable alone—

MARTIN GUERRE

To the Constable, so be it; but that will be, Gabriel, in the presence of the King.

(As he says the name Gabriel, he places his arm around the shoulders of the young man, and the torch which he holds lights Gabriel's face. The prisoner, looking ravished blows them a mute kiss with his two hands joined on his lips.)

CURTAIN

ACT II
SCENE 3

A room in a meeting place for huntsmen in the forest of Saint Germain—at the back, a large door with thick glass, two large windows high up, in cut away. Doors right and left.

The Constable is seated. Arnould du Thil enters by the door at the back. He is dressed exactly as Martin Guerre.

CONSTABLE

Did you meet Madame de Poitiers?

ARNOULD

Yes, Milord, I delivered your letter to her. The hunt is approaching and Madame La Grande Sénéchale is going to try to get here before the King. She asked me, very worried, how it is that you came here alone, abandoning your army.

CONSTABLE

That's good, I'll reply to her. As for you, reply to me. I left you to watch over Gabriel d'Exmes.

ARNOULD

Yes, and Milord owes me 2,000 pounds.

CONSTABLE

Oh! But my son still says, at Paris, that Diana de France left this very day for the Benedictine Convent, bad news for us, and that Mr. d'Exmes was installed near the King as Captain of his guards—good news for our rival.

ARNOULD

That's true, Milord, but as for your rival, I've got him, yes, I possess his most intimate friendship and his most blind confidence.

CONSTABLE

Explain yourself.

ARNOULD

Well, Milord, admire my luck! It seems I resemble to the point of being mistaken for—a certain Martin Guerre, squire, friend and natural brother of the young Vicomte. Same height, same shape and almost the same face. I observe and I study my man from a distance; I learn his voice, his step, his gestures, I had made for myself, at your expense, clothes just like his—and when I choose, Milord, men who detest me to take him for me—and women—who don't detest him—take me for him.

CONSTABLE

Is it possible?

ARNOULD

This Martin Guerre brought up the Vicomte d'Exmes and controls him, I will be able to lead your enemy into a trap, to death, he'll follow me and thank me for it.

CONSTABLE

That would be marvelous!

ARNOULD

And what an amusing game for my malice and my industry to squabble and fight with another me—now there's a pleasure. In the Comic Dreams of Master Rabelais there's a chimera with two heads, one white, one yellow and the yellow head gnaws with all its teeth the head of the pure white head who screams with all his might. I am going to be the yellow head.

CONSTABLE

Yes, you speak true! (the horns signal the arrival) Ah! Ah! The hunt! (going to the door at the back) Madame de Poitiers—oh, but the King is with her, and above all, it's necessary to see her alone.

Come, leave by this way. You will go to Rondpoint to see if a message I'm expecting has arrived.

ARNOULD

And my two thousand pounds?

CONSTABLE

Sure, you'll get them—if you haven't exaggerated your prodigy to me. (they leave by the right)

DIANA DE POITIERS

Why did you leave the hunt so abruptly my dear Sir? What was it that troubled you?

KING

Diana, this forest of Saint Germain bears me ill, I think. Despite all my precautions, I got lost and without knowing how, I found yourself—guess where? At the crossroads of Four Oaks.

DIANA DE POITIERS

Sire—

KING

At that crossroads twenty years ago—I was then, merely Dauphin—the Count de Montgomery was going to be torn apart by a furious stag. I saved his life—only since then I've taken it from him.

DIANA DE POITIERS

It's God that took it from him.

KING

Oh, Madame, I want to believe you, I believe that you didn't love him. But, still, his whole crime was that of loving you—and because I was the son of the King.

DIANA DE POITIERS

My dear lord, leave these cruel recollections—

KING

(sadly) Ah, it's that they don't intend to let me!

DIANA DE POITIERS

Did you always have this soul full of doubt and shadow?

KING

(kissing her hand) Say full of love, my Diana, it's love's flame that casts these shadows.

A PAGE

(at the rear door) Madame Diana of France, arrived from Paris.

KING

Ah, yes! The cruel child who also wants to make me suffer. (to Page) We will receive Madame Diana de France in our arms room. (offering his hand to Diana de Poitiers) Are you coming, sweetie?

DIANA DE POITIERS

(nodding) I'll join Your Majesty, in a minute.

(The King leaves by the door at the left.)

(As soon as the King leaves, the Constable appears at the door on the right.)

CONSTABLE

Diana!

DIANA DE POITIERS

Oh my poor Constable—how confounded you appear. Speak quickly, the King's waiting for me.

CONSTABLE

Diana, the day before yesterday, Saint Laurent's day—the army under my command suffered a horrible defeat on the Plains of Gibercourt. I was myself wounded, made prisoner, I am coming, on parole—to seek money for my ransom.

DIANA DE POITIERS

Oh, my friend! What have I to do?

CONSTABLE

You alone can inform the king of my misfortune.

DIANA DE POITIERS

Well, I'm going to do it instantly.

CONSTABLE

Thanks!

DIANA DE POITIERS

We have never abandoned each other. Still, you cannot be very proud of my power—fragile support which depends on a breath.

The King saw me tremble, just now—his suspicion—after eighteen years—still alive. And the man who can give support to that suspicion is not dead.

CONSTABLE

You are forgetting that he dies if he speaks.

DIANA DE POITIERS

No matter! He has proofs, and so long as he lives, I will tremble. For now, go in there. I am still going to try my best for my old ally, his faithful friend.

CONSTABLE

Diana, to life, to death, count also on me.

(He leaves by the door at the left.)

PAGE

(announcing) Madame Diana de France.

(Diana de France appears at the back accompanied by a Benedictine Sister.)

DIANA DE POITIERS

(hunting) Ah! Madame Diana de France, would do well to wait here until the King has given the order to show her in.

(The two women greet each other coldly; then Diana de Poitiers goes out to the left.)

DIANA de FRANCE

(to herself) Yes, my haughty enemy still intends to place herself between my father's heart and me.

(noticing Gabriel, who enters) Ah, Mr. d'Exmes! You.

GABRIEL

The Captain of the Guards has the privilege of entering here; Gabriel d'Exmes requests the grace of listening to him for a minute.

(Diana makes a sign, the Benedictine withdraws to the rear.)

DIANA de FRANCE

Speak, speak, I am happy at the moment in which I depart to be able to say goodbye to you, for you see I am leaving and the dress of the sister accompanying me tells you where I'm going.

GABRIEL

Well, exactly, you must stay, Diana! You must forget me! You must abandon me to my fate.

DIANA de FRANCE

Gabriel—oh, what have you done?

GABRIEL

Oh, nothing but good, noble, and gentle. But since the day when, under the trees of Mail you delivered this commission to me, a frightful thing has thrown my life into confusion.

DIANA de FRANCE

What is it, my God?

GABRIEL

I cannot tell you everything and I don't know everything myself. But I no longer belong to myself. I belong to battle and to danger.

DIANA de FRANCE

And you are keeping your trouble from me!

GABRIEL

Ah! My most cruel pain is there! Diana, I vowed to you in silence my life and my love. But happily for you, nothing like that binds you.

DIANA de FRANCE

(with a sad smile) Oh—luckily for me.

GABRIEL

Yes, Diana, for my misfortune still separates us; it lets me feel the King is mixed up in this misfortune.

DIANA de FRANCE

My father!

GABRIEL

Thus, my cause won't be yours—not that it may not be just and holy! But it is so difficult and so perilous.

DIANA de FRANCE

Very well! And as for me, I'm only a stranger to you! We didn't grow up orphans together! And precisely because I am the daughter of the King, I cannot even try to intervene between my father and you.

GABRIEL

Diana, let me keep my courage! Think, will you! At the first opportunity today, now the struggle can begin for me, an unequal struggle, in which I will have to risk so much, suffer so much!

DIANA de FRANCE

Why then, you intend to test me, do you! Why for little that one who has an elevated soul don't you know that danger invites and peril attracts! Ah, you've been so devoted to me, ingrate! And you expect me to be indifferent! Ah, you are bad, evil! And you forbid me to console you, to help you! Ah, that's the way it is! Well, no, you shared your joys with me, as for me, I intend to be with you in your sorrows! Ah, you suffer! Well! I love you!

GABRIEL

My adored Diana!

PAGE

(entering from the left) The king informs Madame de France, that he's going to come find her here. Milord Captain of the Guards, His Majesty directs you to convoke in this hall all the gentlemen and captains present at St. Germain.

DIANA de FRANCE

The King! Go, Gabriel! Go.

(Gabriel wildly kisses Diana's hand and leaves by the back—a moment later the King enters.)

KING

Before our chat, my daughter, you need to know—you are going to know—why, at this moment less than ever, it is permissible for us to take back our word to the Constable.

DIANA de FRANCE

Sire, less than ever, also, I have to right to dispose of my life.

KING

Ah, I love you, Diana, and you desolate me.

DIANA de FRANCE

Sire, I love you, why will you make me despair?

KING

You persist in your wish to return to the Benedictines?

DIANA de FRANCE

The carriage that must take me there is awaiting me.

KING

In any case, it cannot be to the Benedictines of Saint Quentin.

DIANA de FRANCE

The Saintly Mother Church, who brought me up still resides at Saint Quentin. Why can I not go rejoin her?

KING

You are going to learn with all our gentlemen.

(Enter the Gentlemen and Captains—among them Gabriel and Guerre, from the left. Diana de Poitiers is accompanied by several ladies—)

KING

Come, gentlemen, I am going to announce sorrowful news to you, sooner made to excite French souls than to beat them down. We have a great revenge to take. The army commanded by our Constable was defeated the day before yesterday in the environs of Saint Quentin.

(The Constable enters from the right.)

CONSTABLE

(bending his knee) Sire—

KING

(raising him) Cousin, you have to bend your knee only before God. Battle depends on men—victory alone depends on God. We will no longer think of this defeat but on means of repairing it.

CONSTABLE

Sire, I don't wish to hide anything from Your Majesty. The army is almost destroyed and the road to Paris open to the enemy. The town of Saint Quentin that the Spaniards are besieging can alone, by prolonging its resistance, stop the march of the conquerors. Unfortunately, it isn't fortified. To reassemble the remnants of our army will require at least a week, and my nephew Coligny, who has valiantly thrown himself into the place, was not sure, on my departure, of being able to hold it for two days.

KING

And you have not had, since then, news of him?

CONSTABLE

I am awaiting it, Sire. (looking about for Arnould de Thil and noting Martin Guerre) Ah! There you are! Well, you've informed yourself of this message?

MARTIN GUERRE

(astonished) Milord Constable mistakes me; my name is Martin Guerre. I belong to Mr. d'Exmes.

CONSTABLE

(looking at him, surprised) Ah! Yes. (aside)—Arnould didn't deceive me, strange resemblance. (A page comes to present him with a letter.)

But here's this letter, Sire. (at a gesture from the King he opens it and scans it) The Admiral demands men and especially officers. If they cannot be sent, he cannot answer for the ability to hold Saint Quentin more than forty-eight hours.

KING

Ah! Saint Quentin! Saint Quentin! It's there at the fortune of France lies—Saint Quentin, my good town, if you hold only eight days, the defense of the territory can be organized behind your faithful walls. Ah, for each of your hours of resistance, I will give you a privilege, and for each of your collapsed stones, a diamond. Eight days! Eight days! Who then will make Saint Quentin hold out for eight days?

MARTIN GUERRE

(in a low voice within a group) Why, it's possible!

KING

(turning) Who spoke? (silence) Eh, if one of you, gentlemen, has something to say, let him speak, let him speak quickly! In the present peril, we will loan our ear to the lowest pikeman in our army.

MARTIN GUERRE

Sire, a humble soldier can have the audacity to raise his voice?

KING

(signaling him to approach) Who are you?

MARTIN GUERRE

The Squire of your Captain of the Guards, Sire. My Lord is so modest! He does not dare speak aloud the idea—oh, a proud idea—which he shared with me in a whisper.

KING

Mr. d'Exmes was the right arm of Mr. de Guerre at the siege of Metz—so what was his idea?

MARTIN GUERRE

Your Majesty promised everything to a city which would defend itself—for sure he will grant as much to the men who would defend it?

KING

Yes, whatever he requests of me—all!

MARTIN GUERRE

Ah! It's because this man may not be the first to come, at least he would have to impose his will and his courage on a city completely; and during eight days endure tests and shocks. But all the same, this man, I know him, as for me, I've seen him work for six years. Ah! He won't flinch, he won't even fall back! No more in the impossible than in the possible! And this man, with the permission of Your Majesty, is quite simply his Captain of Guards.

CONSTABLE

(shrugging his shoulders) He's crazy!

KING

Still, he undertook to hold Saint Quentin—if he gave us eight days. Ah—leave us with Mr. d'Exmes and his Squire.

(the Lords present withdraw—the King approaches Diana de

France)

KING

Diana, you see why it is impossible for you to return to the Benedictines of Saint Quentin?

DIANA de FRANCE

Because there will be wounded and dying? That reason doesn't suffice for your daughter, father.

KING

Go in there, and don't leave until our audience with Mr. d'Exmes.

DIANA de FRANCE

(aside) Oh—Gabriel's secret—I intend to know it, I shall know it.

(She leaves by the right.)

GABRIEL

(low to Martin Guerre) Are you really thinking about what you are risking?

MARTIN GUERRE

No—I am thinking only of what I intend to gain.

KING

Mr. d'Exmes, speak, do you really think you can prolong the defense of our brave city for a week? In that case, demand from us, at your whim, favor, dignities, titles, riches.

GABRIEL

More or less than all that, Sire.

DIANA DE POITIERS

(low to Constable) It's clear the hand of Diana de France.

GABRIEL

Sire, what I solicit is not a favor, it's a pardon.

KING

A pardon?

GABRIEL

Yes, Sire, mercy for a condemned.

KING

And who is this condemned?

GABRIEL

My father.

KING

Your father, Mr. d'Exmes? I didn't know you still had a father.

GABRIEL

Two weeks ago, I didn't know it either.

KING

Ah—and what is the penalty that your father is subject to?

GABRIEL

The harshest captivity.

DIANA DE POITIERS

(low to the Constable) What's he talking about?

KING

His crime must then have been grave? What was his crime?

GABRIEL

I don't know how to answer that, question, Sire.

KING

And why, sir, do you want to be silent to me as to the truth?

GABRIEL

My God! I am unaware of part of it myself.

KING

You are unaware of it?

GABRIEL

One man alone knows it completely.

KING

And who is that man?

GABRIEL

(embarrassed) Sire, I think there's perhaps a mortal secret about it—and I cannot name that man even to Your Majesty.

MARTIN GUERRE

(advancing) Well! Why's that? I'm that man.

KING

You—what! You've so long hidden so grave a secret from your master?

MARTIN GUERRE

Sire, I owe it to him. But today, I am ready to reveal it before Your Majesty.

CONSTABLE

Take care, friend! Mr. d'Exmes admits to us himself that there might be some boldness in your revelations. You are sure of what you are going to put forward. You have proof.

MARTIN GUERRE

Oh! I've got better than proof, Mr. Constable, I've got witnesses.

KING

Come on! Speak in that case, speak.

MARTIN GUERRE

Well, Sire, one night, eighteen years ago—

DIANA DE POITIERS

(shivering) Eighteen years.

MARTIN GUERRE

I entered my service in the room of the Lord whose page I was. Oh, I loved him and he loved me. It must be said—I was the child of a love of his youth. He crumpled a letter, he was very pale and he said in a whisper, "We'll never laugh again."

He rose, he took his sword, he embraced his young son, who was sleeping, and he left. I rejoined him at the door of the house, he forbade me to go any further. But I realized little by little where he was going ,and even what sorrow and what danger; and I followed him despite his prohibition.

KING

But first of all, his name? The name of your master? Why are you omitting to say his name?

MARTIN GUERRE

Sire, his name is the Count of Montgomery.

KING and DIANA

(at the same time) Montgomery!

(Gabriel, distracted, shakes Martin Guerre's hand.)

CONSTABLE

Does the King wish to hear any more?

KING

Wait, Constable—Mr. d'Exmes, I thought the one of whom you were going to speak to us was your father?

MARTIN GUERRE

The Vicomte d'Exmes is one of the appanages of his family, and he had the right to take the title—but his name is Montgomery.

DIANA DE POITIERS

Sire, it is at least useless to recall this unfortunate history before those who are here.

MARTIN GUERRE

I ask your pardon, Madame, there are two persons here who do not know this complete story—my master and the King.

KING

(stupefied) Me, you say?

DIANA DE POITIERS

Sire, don't suffer—

MARTIN GUERRE

Ah—the King has deigned to question me, Madame.

CONSTABLE

Well, speak in that case, but take care!

MARTIN GUERRE

Of what? Of my life? Oh, I know very well that I risked it. I have only one support—justice—and only one strength—the truth.

KING

But in the presence of the King that suffices.

MARTIN GUERRE

That's actually what I believed, Sire, and I don't find myself so audacious. (turning towards Gabriel) Mr. d'Exmes, I went there despite your father, Madame Diana de Poitiers, the Constable, Milord the Dauphin, today the King, who hears me.

CONSTABLE

Eh! But apparently you were there, too, were you?

MARTIN GUERRE

Yes, truly, sir, I was there, hidden, all atremble behind a tapestry. Oh! you will have forgotten the insignificant detail of a young unknown man, who that night made the senseless attempt to free the count, and who was surprised, struck, and left for dead on the spot. Well, he wasn't dead; it's he who speaks to you.

CONSTABLE

Sire, do you permit—?

MARTIN GUERRE

But, sir, allow me then to speak, since the King wants to hear me. At my appeal, my master was carried away by a sort of storm of passion and fury. He affirmed that Madame de Poitiers had accepted him as her suitor and fiancé.

"He isn't anymore," shouted the Dauphin of France! "There's only a man who calls himself the fiancé of the woman that I love."

And he admonished Madame Diana and he insulted the Constable, and he dared, yes, Milord, he dared to provoke the son of the King. The son of the King drew his sword, the Constable rushed between them.

All this, for me was confused, breathless, doleful like a dream, and the outbursts of voices, the agitated steps, the very silences even gave me a sort of terrible vision that acted on me like a fever.

When at last—(he hesitates)

KING

(rising) When at least you heard the Dauphin shout to the Constable, "Let him alone! Leave us alone!" His glove grazed my face, he must now kill me or I must kill him!

MARTIN GUERRE

Yes, I heard it, that honest and royal shout, and I bear witness to it, and you would have, Mr. d'Exmes, remembered it eternally; it is the role of the Dauphin of France.

GABRIEL

Oh, Sire—

MARTIN GUERRE

Madame de Poitiers also uttered a scream, but naturally, less heroic, it was to call the men escorting the Prince. In a minute, my dear master was gagged, garroted, and taken away. The Dauphin protested, opposing himself to it, all ashiver with rage and also jealousy.

He said, "Who knows, after all, if this man lied, if he's not loved?" The Constable said, "The proof will be easy and prompt. In your opinion, Madame Diana, what ought we to do with this man who just so outraged the son of the King?"

Madame Diana replied, "What is the penalty for crimes of lèse majesté—death, I believe? My opinion then is that this man should die?"

And the Constable shouted, "It seems to me, Prince, that Madame is justified! But no judgment is possible. The insult, to remain secret, demands a secret punishment. The guilty party must neither die nor live; he must disappear!" And Milord Constable courageously took the disappearance upon himself. Have I said the truth?

CONSTABLE

I'm not thinking of denying it.

MARTIN GUERRE

Well, I have promised that I would produce my witnesses—you've heard them, Milord, the King first. Now, as to what the King is unaware of, in your turn be witness.

KING

Yes, tell us what you know, Vicomte d'Exmes.

GABRIEL

Pardon, Sire! I'm no longer calling myself Vicomte d'Exmes.

KING

Well! Speak Count Montgomery.

GABRIEL

I am not the Count of Montgomery either.

KING

What? Who are you then?

GABRIEL

I am the Vicomte de Montgomery.

KING

God! You imagine that your father is not dead?

GABRIEL

No question, since I am asking for his pardon. He is living, Sire! He is living.

KING

Living! Ah, on honor, they have hidden it from me.

MARTIN GUERRE

On honor, I was sure of it.

GABRIEL

Sire, I have seen, I have touched my father, but he's dying for the last eighteen years—in a captivity that would frighten a hangman.

CONSTABLE

(threatening) Sir!

MARTIN GUERRE

(shocked, to Gabriel) Oh, don't tell—don't say what this capacity is! Rather I, it's I who—

KING

No—get it over with sir, finish without fear.

GABRIEL

Sire, imagine the torture. Each time the prisoner merely tries to utter a word, he is condemned to a darker, harsher cell—twice already he's descended these platforms of hell—

MARTIN GUERRE

The last will be a tomb!

KING

Oh! Constable! Constable!

MARTIN GUERRE

Here's what happened, Sire, and you know nothing about it. It's evident, if you had known of it, one day, one hour, one minute, it would not have happened—for example, while looking at your son, you would have thought of this wretched father.

Then you would have placed in the balance the sin and the crime, and taking good measure, you would have said, "That's enough now." But no. Between the pity of those who judge and the suffering of those who expiate, there must always be, intercepting clemency and overriding pardon—between those complacent about torture and those rushing to punish!

KING

How do you respond, Mr. Constable?

DIANA DE POITIERS

Milord Constable, allow me to reply for you and for myself.

KING

(terrified) You, Madame, you!

DIANA DE POITIERS

Yes, Sire, me, for I acted in concert with the Constable. We wanted, he and I, to spare Your Majesty's heart even the shadow of a care— And we took upon ourselves responsibility for this just and necessary punishment.

KING

God!

DIANA DE POITIERS

It seems that our zeal was culpable? Right! But what? Why, today the King has only to free the Count de Montgomery; all will be restored to him, the odium of tortures past will fall on us alone; and they will say of you, Sire, "O the Great, the just Prince, who's pardoned those who outraged him and punished those who loved him!"

KING

It's true—what to do?—Oh! There's an invincible fatality to it, and seems as impossible to pardon as to punish.

GABRIEL

Sire! Act! Don't talk like that! Why, one would say that you are no longer thinking of the great ransom that I am proposing to you. A city for a man. The defense of Saint Quentin will save France—is it too high a price to save my father?

Sire, God helping me, I shall succeed. I will hold Saint Quentin, eight, ten, a dozen days. Yes, I will do that, and yet more— Yes, for the previous liberty that I demand—it's very little to delay the taking of a city. Well, Sire, speak the order and I will conquer another.

MARTIN GUERRE

(low to Gabriel) Child—that's a word too many.

DIANA DE POITIERS

He's bold, that young man. (low, to Constable)

KING

Well, look, my cousin, you yourself, it seems to me, you are touched.

CONSTABLE

The man is touched, Sire, the minister is not convinced. The promise demanded is serous. Wanting to preserve the kingdom, let's not compromise the King.

MARTIN GUERRE

Eh! Milord Constable, you who calculate so carefully, how can you ignore the most likely result? Mr. d'Exmes spoke with the intoxication of his age—but in this desperate enterprise don't you see that we are going—that we intend—to die.

DIANA DE POITIERS

(low to Constable) Listen!

MARTIN GUERRE

(to Gabriel) Yes, my dear lord, have no illusion, Saint Quentin may resist or succumb, we will remain on that breach we are going to defend. But what matter! We will be quit of our duty as the King will be quit of his debt.

DIANA DE POITIERS

(low to Constable) He's right!

CONSTABLE

(low to Diana) And I have a means to assist the chances of mortality. (aloud) Well, Sire?

KING

Well?

CONSTABLE

If Mr. d'Exmes and his squire, who are there in possession of a formidable state secret, can attest on oath that, for one thing, they alone know this secret and that they will not reveal it to anyone in this world until after their work is accomplished.

GABRIEL

I swear it. (extending his hand, Martin Guerre extends his in silence)

CONSTABLE

That being so, I find it is impossible to deal rigorously with so much courage and devotion. Yes, Sire, you, you ought, Sire, to give to Mr. d'Exmes your word in exchange for his.

KING

Ah! God be praised! I breathe. (to Gabriel) Keep then, Mr. d'Exmes, your valiant promises. I give my word as a gentleman and King that I will do what you wish.

CONSTABLE

(who has filled out and signed a parchment) Here, sir, is your commission for Saint Quentin.

GABRIEL

Ah, Sire! Thanks, thanks!

MARTIN GUERRE

Come on then, come, my dear lord, and you will thank the King better—on your return from Saint Quentin, for, at bottom, I keep some hope, Mr. Constable, that we will return from there—both of us.

CURTAIN

ACT II
SCENE 4

Saint Quentin. Rear courtyard of the lodging of Jean Peuquoy. To the right, the home, to the left, a shed. Facing the audience, a high wall with an exterior gate about three-quarters demolished. At the back, the town completely devastated and ruined by the bombardment; at the left houses half collapsed, debris of ramparts to the right, large breaches everywhere.

Night—the cannons echo in the distance at regular intervals, streaks of red light burst from time to time over the horizon.

Jean Peuquoy, Pillemiche, and Babette emerge from the house.

PILLEMICHE

What! Nobody at your place has seen Martin Guerre tonight?

BABETTE

My God! No. And Macette or myself were always awake.

JEAN

You dreamed, Pillemiche! Martin Guerre is dead. Quite dead.

PILLEMICHE

Whatever the devil may be, I still spoke to him—I helped him to get into Saint Quentin. He asked where your lodging was, I indicated to him the other gate, on the Rue des Filandieres.

JEAN

But why didn't he go find Mr. d'Exmes at the breach?

PILLEMICHE

He told me he was too tired.

JEAN

Him, tired? Martin Guerre! Pillemiche either you were sleeping standing or you have that annoying infirmity called—

PILLEMICHE

Called what?

JEAN

Called delusional. But come quick to rejoin Mr. d'Exmes. Oh! the brave young man! With the reinforcements he brought us, with the ardor and cleverness with which he deployed them, he's preserved the city up to now! And yet, I have the idea that if he is unsuccessful in holding it at least one day more, he's determined to get himself killed on the last standing section of the wall. (looking toward the town) Ah! The Benedictine Sisters who are going to ambulances.

(At the back can be seen eight or more Benedictines in white and blue habits preceded by men of the people with torches.)

BABETTE

I'm going to join them, brother.

JEAN

Go, child, go.

(Babette goes out to join the Benedictines) And look, always at the head, Diana de France. Saint Quentin was already desperate when she got here. The King thought she was going to the Benedictines of Orleans, but she turned to the direction of danger.

And day and night she's there, this daughter of France, watching, consoling, curing. In the convent they call her Sister Benedicta, but our poor folks don't know Latin, they call her simply Sister Blessed—and that's better than Madame Duchess. On that note, Pillemiche, to the ramparts!

(A dozen bourgeois armed pass running at the back)

PILLEMICHE

Hey, Jean—that looks like your company.

JEAN

Heavens! Why yes—(raising his voice) Hola! Where are you going, the rest of you?

FIRST BOURGEOIS

The Breach of Saint André has been taken.

SECOND BOURGEOIS

Mr. de Coligny is sending us to Fort Saint Jean. Is it necessary to go there?

FIRST BOURGEOIS

Why do it? It's all over.

JEAN

(head lowered) Yes, it's all over! For the last five days, the enemy left us in peace, but they certainly thought that the first assault would be the last! We don't have one whole wall left to us, not a tower standing; our poor Saint Quentin is floored like a soldier who's been well beaten, and we are lost, it's evident, without remission and without hope.

FIRST BOURGEOIS

Yes, yes, we must surrender.

ALL

We've got to surrender.

JEAN

(astonished, raising his head) Why no—are they dumb! We must die!

ALL

Die!

JEAN

Well, yes! Good-for-nothing! Mr. de Coligny and Mr. d'Exmes will show us how it must be done. Our stories will give us a good example. Fort Saint Jean still holds. (taking from the hands of a young boy the flag with the town's arms) To Fort Saint Jeans!

ALL

To Fort Saint Jean! (they leave)

MACETTE

(emerging from the house) Martin Guerre! You can come.

(Arnould de Thil emerges with caution, wrapped in his cloak.)

ARNOULD

(disguising his voice) Goodbye. I'm rushing to danger!

MACETTE

(retaining him) Bah! You've got plenty of time. Tonight, instead of going to let yourself be lynched by others. You finally let yourself be kept by your Macette, here you are in truth. Think, then, my Martin Guerre. I can call you my Martin Guerre now. Think that I thought you dead, that I saw you hanged.

ARNOULD

Tell me that again.

MACETTE

(astonished) For the second time?

ARNOULD

(stamping his foot) Again, I tell you!

MACETTE

Ah! Fine! Very Fine! (aside) Right, he talks like a master! (aloud) You remember—for at that moment, you had all your head—that arriving at Saint Quentin, we all fell, you, me, Pillemiche, in a bivouac of Flemings. Those brutes took you for a Renaud—Arnould—I don't know any more. They told us later that this Renaud had just escaped from them, carrying off a certain Gudule, the wife of their Captain.

(Arnould laughs, turning away.)

MACETTE

They asked you—Gudule? What did you do with Gudule? As if you were capable, poor innocent. After that, now, I don't know much.

(Arnould stamps his foot.)

MACETTE

In short, my Martin Guerre, I saw these furious men garrote you, and prepare the hanging noose. Then I fainted but Pillemiche, he saw the end, he saw you hoisted and hung from an oak.

ARNOULD

And dead? Actually dead?

MACETTE

Eh! Yes—he thought so at the least, but at last, my Martin Guerre, they unhung you in time?

ARNOULD

(impatiently) By Jove! And my young master?

MACETTE

Mr. d'Exmes! Oh the news of your death put him in despair and he fought like someone who really wanted to follow you, my Martin Guerre.

ARNOULD

Ah! You bore me with your Martin Guerre.

MACETTE

Ingrate. You would like to frighten me! But no, hold on, I am even more jealous of that little Babette who offends me, a bit, because you please her, dear man, and because in the end, she's actually richer than me.

ARNOULD

(cocking his ear) You say?

MACETTE

Ah, someone's coming—

ARNOULD

(who's glanced down the street) Go inside!

MACETTE

Eh, but if you—

ARNOULD

(angrily shoving her) Go inside, will you?

MACETTE

I obey, my friend, I obey. (to herself) Ah! But what a man now! How the gibbet profited him. (she goes into the house)

ARNOULD

(alone, looking back) Long live me! It looks like that little Babette. As for her, I will actually marry her dowry. Later, your affairs, dear Constable! I am in luck on my own score.

(Babette enters.)

ARNOULD

Dear cousin.

BABETTE

(with a cry of joy) Ah! My cousin Martin Guerre! So it's actually true! You are not dead?

ARNOULD

Babette. (he opens his arms to her)

BABETTE

Ah! Leave me alone! How quickly shall I run to announce you to Mr. d'Exmes! He's just been wounded!

ARNOULD

Wounded!

BABETTE

In the shoulder. Not dangerously, they are bringing him here. Oh, he'll be so happy to know.

ARNOULD

(trying to attract her to him) No; stay—above all—one kisses one's cousin—pretty little thing.

BABETTE

(recoiling) Ah! How you say that to me?

ARNOULD

I said it ill?

BABETTE

You said it somewhat boldly—

ARNOULD

(smiling) And that troubles you?

BABETTE

No, that offends me.

ARNOULD

Oh! Oh! You weren't so shy in Paris!

BABETTE

In Paris you were so timid! You almost seemed afraid of me, then, as for me, I had no fear of you.

ARNOULD

And you no longer find me the same?

BABETTE

No, I don't know if it's being in the country that is changing you—

ARNOULD

Child! Come on, look, a little kiss!

BABETTE

(recoiling) No.

ARNOULD

Still, you've given me many kisses already.

BABETTE

Much better! I asked you for 'em. Yes, sometimes I'd say, "Kiss me, will you, cousin!" You approached a bit clumsily with your nice brotherly look, respectful and tender, and you gave me a sweet kiss on the face—which didn't embarrass me. But, now, I don't know when you say to me—"A little kiss" your gesture, your voice, seem so mocking—and I become red—and I want to cry and hold on. Leave me alone, I prefer to escape, I'm ashamed. (she quickly goes into the house)

ARNOULD

Look at that little prude! Hum! The devil's withdrawing from my game. So let's get back to that of the Constable. (looking around toward the back) Mr. d'Exmes! Whereabouts is he? Massacre! Isn't that Diana de France who accompanies him? Let's have a bit of a look.

(He hides in the corner of the house.)

(Dawn begins to rise. The cannon echoes still at regular intervals.)

(Jean Peuquoy and another bourgeois enter supporting Gabriel, wounded. Diana de France and another Benedictine sister accompany them.)

JEAN

Sister Blessed, he's losing consciousness.

DIANA de FRANCE

Place him there on that stone. He will revive more quickly in fresh air.

(They set Gabriel on the debris of a wall. The second Bourgeois leaves. Diana examines the wound.)

DIANA de FRANCE

Ah, the dressing is out of order. Help me, sister—

JEAN

Is the wound dangerous?

DIANA de FRANCE

No, the danger isn't there. (going close to Jean) But this wound will be a terrible blow if Saint Quentin cannot resist another day.

JEAN

(slowly shaking his head) Yes, I suspect so, but—

DIANA de FRANCE

Mr. de Coligny has not capitulated, right?

JEAN

No, sister Blessed, although you hear the cannon—we are still hanging on—but I'm actually afraid you won't hear it much longer.

(Gabriel supported by this sister, stirs.)

DIANA de FRANCE

Hush! He's opening his eyes.

JEAN

I am going in the house to see if everything is prepared to receive him. (to Benedictine) Come, Sister. (they go into the house)

GABRIEL

(coming to) Diana?

DIANA de FRANCE

Don't talk!

GABRIEL

Why's that?

DIANA de FRANCE

(to herself) It seems to me that the noise of the cannon has ceased.

GABRIEL

Ah! I remember—a wound.

DIANA de FRANCE

(to herself) I don't hear a thing anymore.

GABRIEL

Has it been a long while that I fainted?

DIANA de FRANCE

No—a few minutes. (aside) Not a thing!

GABRIEL

What are you listening to. (uttering a cry) Ah! I understand. Silence!

DIANA de FRANCE

Gabriel!

GABRIEL

(in despair) Saint Quentin has capitulated!

DIANA de FRANCE

Gabriel! Look, if that is the case, this town, so weak, this open place has, nonetheless, thanks to you, held out for twelve whole days.

GABRIEL

No, Diana, no! Saint Quentin resisted for twelve days, but it's not I who came to the honor of this defense. On the last five days, someone outside—Mr. de Guise, the Constable, how do I know—someone has occupied the enemy with powerful diversions—and thus preserve the town. But as for me, I promised the king eight days and I really held it only seven.

DIANA de FRANCE

Oh! And you imagine the King is going to demand so strictly the accomplishment of your word?

GABRIEL

Ah, Diana, you cannot know and I am forbidden to tell you what in exchange with my undertaking fulfilled, the King owes me in his turn.

DIANA de FRANCE

(aside) I know all the same.

GABRIEL

But my work incomplete is nothing and doesn't count. I have nothing to demand of the King! Nothing! Ah! From today, I've forever lost rest and joy.

DIANA de FRANCE

Gabriel, oh, but I am here. I wanted to be here precisely for this hour of trial, to console your discouragement as well as to dress your wounds. Oh! I beg you, don't be so cruel, don't suffer so much—keep hoping.

GABRIEL

Ah! Diana, the more adorable you are the more unfortunate I am! See all that I have lost at the same time; first of all the sacred and mysterious object of my pursuits and my efforts; that I don't know what blessed illusion murmured in the depth of my heart that perhaps, after the victory perhaps—conquer even you and deserve you—and fate has not even left me the one who in action was my adviser and my support, my brother Martin Guerre is dead!

BABETTE

(who just entered) Not so, Milord, he's alive.

GABRIEL

Alive!

BABETTE

Eh! Yes, he was here just now.

GABRIEL

Martin Guerre! Yes, indeed, they swore that to me already. But where is he? (dolorously) Why didn't he come to me right away?

BABETTE

They're going looking for him.

DIANA de FRANCE

But we have to go inside and wait for him in the house.

BABETTE

Lean on us.

GABRIEL

Ah! I've found my strength and my courage.

DIANA de FRANCE

Was I right to advise you to hope?

GABRIEL

Yes, what an angel promises, it's God who fulfills it!

(they go into the house)

ARNOULD

(alone, revealing himself) Eh! Why, he seems in a very bad way, the enemy of my Constable! Let's carry him to his false Martin Guerre. And then, once I've got the real one hung in my place—I shall not tell the boss too much bad news. (noise in the distance.) There's the English, the Piedmontese, the Flemish making their entry into Saint Quentin. The poor town is going to resemble the tower of Babel. Bah! Let's hide from this confusion.

(He heads for the street as a troop of enemies pass by running at the back. Jack Tobin detaches himself from them and accosts Arnould.)

JACK TOBIN

(with a thick English accent) Oh! I see you again already?

ARNOULD

Huh? You know me, my dear fellow?

JACK TOBIN

Yes, quite well! You are Martin Guerre who was hanged and

unhanged?

ARNOULD

Heavens, yes, he knows me. Goodbye.

JACK TOBIN

Hello! I choose your presence.

ARNOULD

Me! And by what right? From what country are you? English it seems to me?

JACK TOBIN

From Calais! I am justly proud to still be with the conquerors. Today I am English in the English town guard, and English merchant. My name is Jack Tobin. I pronounce it Jacques Tobin when I march with your French fellow citizens—but when my English compatriots are stronger, I pronounce it Jack Tobin!

ARNOULD

That's frank. But that doesn't tell me why I am your prisoner.

JACK TOBIN

You know the terms of the capitulation?

ARNOULD

No.

JACK TOBIN

Saint Quentin must furnish 100 prisoners at the choice of our captains who will get ransom paid for them. Lord Grey, the governor of Calais and my Lord has for his share a gentleman and a bourgeois—he directed me, for a cash reward, to choose those of good quality.

ARNOULD

Ah! Ah! A gentleman and a bourgeois.

JACK TOBIN

Yes, and I'm choosing you—with a bourgeois face.

ARNOULD

Thanks! But tell me—if your chosen—by chance do not have money for their ransom them,—what will you do with 'em?

JACK TOBIN

We are taking them prisoners to Calais.

ARNOULD

Ah! You are taking them—My! My! My! I thought I was going to bring back to the Constable all good news. Would you like, Jack Tobin, for me to make you an offer?

JACK TOBIN

Oh, yes—I understand offers like this very well.

ARNOULD

Suppose I point out to you a prisoner—a noble with 10,000 pounds?

JACK TOBIN

Oh—what's his name—where is he?

ARNOULD

He's in that house. His name is the Vicomte d'Exmes.

JACK TOBIN

Oh—I know—very good noble and you—you, very good bourgeois.

ARNOULD

No, me bad! Me, poor squire—but if I were to offer you in my place, a big bourgeois with a thousand crowns?

JACK TOBIN

Name him, point him out.

ARNOULD

Jean Peuquoy, master weaver. Still in that house.

JACK TOBIN

The nephew of my Captain Pierre Peuquoy. Fine! Right fine! Thanks! Oh—why I remember Martin Guerre, sir! The Vicomte d'Exmes is your lord and Jean Peuquoy is your relative—I heard you say that to Mr. de Coligny just now?

ARNOULD

Me! I said just now.

JACK TOBIN

Yes, in the town hall.

ARNOULD

In the town hall?

JACK TOBIN

Yes, when you told how you'd been hanged and unhanged.

ARNOULD

I was telling—thunder and lightning! The real Martin Guerre was really unhanged.

JACK TOBIN

What are you saying?

ARNOULD

I say—I say—Jack Tobin that you are my savior! I say that I have a good horse and the route to Paris is beautiful! I say that having been hanged and unhanged, I don't wish under any pretext to be rehanged.

(he leaves running)

JACK TOBIN

(alone, to himself) Oh, I don't understand that gentleman—but he seems to me to understand business horribly well—ah! My Captain and one of my prisoners. (he steps to the side)

(Enter Jean Peuquoy, Pierre Peuquoy helmeted, emerging from the house.)

PIERRE

Let's leave the women, nephew, Jean, and let's talk.

JEAN

(striding around agitatedly) Ah! Uncle, this Martin Guerre! Why is it Macette and Babette have so much against him? Must he add more to our chagrins on such a day! My poor old city. Uncle Pierre, here I am, like you, Spanish or English, I don't know exactly but you always have more to make me jealous of being gay.

PIERRE

Who knows, Jean—if the two of us won't become gay again together. (to Tobin, who advances and bows) Hey, Jack Tobin, what are you doing here?

JACK TOBIN

My Captain, take in good part what I have to tell you. Your nephew, Jean Peuquoy is prisoner of Lord Grey at the ransom of a thousand crowns, and until this is paid, he'll be taken prisoner to Calais.

JEAN

Me, prisoner?

PIERRE

Him to Calais.

JACK TOBIN

The other prisoner of Lord Gray is Mr. d'Exmes and I'm going to notify him of the news.

PIERRE

Oh, Tobin—one single word! Who is it who invented these two prisoners? Who is it who made this fine double hit?

JACK TOBIN

By God! It's your relative, Martin Guerre. (he goes into the house)

JEAN

Again Martin Guerre! Oh! This is too much.

PIERRE

(running his hand) Yes, Jean, you are right, this is too much! This goes above something! I don't know what this is, but this must be something excellent. There's my great idea which germinates and sprouts up! Saint Quentin is taken, that's certain. It's necessary that it be retaken, and that Calais be retaken in the bargain.

JEAN

This Martin Guerre, I am sure he intends to get me away from here, but I am going to pay the thousand crowns.

PIERRE

Be careful indeed, wretch! You are forgetting Fort Risbank. I will lead you to Calais, Mr. d'Exmes and you, like the maneuver of Providence. (solemnly) Weaver, I have an order to give you.

JEAN

What order!

PIERRE

Hush! A ladder—a ladder—a big rope ladder.

JEAN

That's fine. But if you believe Martin Guerre is in your plan—

PIERRE

I don't know about that. Perhaps he didn't know himself.

(Macette and Babette emerge from the house.)

JEAN

I tell you, that he's a turncoat and a liar.

MACETTE

(who's overheard) Oh! yes, a liar—oh! I've just talked with

Babette. And you haven't seen him again, the swindler?

PIERRE

No, not yet.

BABETTE

And Mr. d'Exmes begins to get impatient and angry with him.

JEAN

Ah! Hold on, it's him. At last.

PIERRE

Look at him come—

MARTIN GUERRE

(to himself) (noticing Pierre and Jean—he enters from the back) How astonished and happy they are going to be. How they are going to receive me with joyful hearts. Am I moved! They don't see me. They seem very serious.

(coughing) Hum, hum! They don't hear me. (Deciding and coming forward, aloud)

Well! It's me.

JEAN

Ah! It's you.

MARTIN GUERRE

Yes, me, Martin Guerre—it looks like you don't recognize me.

PIERRE

Yes, it's true, you've changed greatly, Martin Guerre.

MARTIN GUERRE

Ah! That's still not a reason to receive me so coldly. I've indeed had troubles and setbacks. If you knew! I have again paid for another. I was ill to death for a whole week. For the last five days. I'm better, for goodness sakes, I think in five days I'm going to be well enough. Ah, indeed! But you are not replying to me. You are not looking at me. Look, what have you got against me?

JEAN

And Babette! And Macette! What is it they have against you, Martin Guerre?

MARTIN GUERRE

Babette? Macette?

PIERRE

Yes, they are there, complaining about you together, but refusing to tell us anything.

MACETTE

Only Babette's blushing.

MARTIN GUERRE

My dear little Babette!

BABETTE

And Macette's weeping.

MARTIN GUERRE

My poor Macette!

JEAN

And Mr. d'Exmes, your young lord, wounded, why do you seem to avoid and flee him?

MARTIN GUERRE

Me! Gabriel!

PIERRE

How were you able to say to Pillemiche, you—that you were too tired to fight?

MARTIN GUERRE

Ah! Look here, who is it who's crazy here, you or me?

PIERRE

At last, to what incomprehensible purpose—because for that thing I cannot suppose you guilty—but from what bizarre idea did you denounce—to be led as prisoners to Calais—who? Your cousin Jean and Mr. d'Exmes—your master?

MARTIN GUERRE

Oh! Why do you want to make me damned, Uncle? And first of all, when did I comment on all these infamies—?

JEAN

Why since last midnight when you were here.

MARTIN GUERRE

Since midnight! But I just got here. I entered Saint Quentin only a half hour ago.

BABETTE and MACETTE

Oh!

JEAN

Come off it! Pillemiche, Tobin, Macette, Babette saw you and spoke to you.

MARTIN GUERRE

Ah! My God!

JEAN

What's wrong with him?

MARTIN GUERRE

A suspicion! A terrible suspicion—which already came to me in Paris in the last time, when they accused me of all sorts of immodest and abominable actions the mere telling of which made me tremble.

PIERRE

What suspicion?

MARTIN GUERRE

One of two things. Either I am possessed, possessed by a devil—and there are times when I belong to him without knowing it—or I have a double, a perverse and cheating likeness—another form of Satan.

JEAN

Is it possible?

MARTIN GUERRE

Hey! Praise God—is it easier to imagine me, one who did so much—that is to say who did nothing at all, but at least who ever and everywhere followed Milord protecting him, I mean obeying him like a faithful dog, is it possible to admit that I suddenly became from morn to midnight, a Cain and a Judas?

(Gabriel emerges from the house.)

MARTIN GUERRE

(rushing to Gabriel) Ah, my dear child, my good young master! Come, come protect me.

GABRIEL

(with a shout of joy) Ah! (in a tone of tender reproach) It's you! It's you at last!

MARTIN GUERRE

At last? Then it's true, you were asking for me and I didn't come! Oh! And you have the look of being angry, too.

GABRIEL

Me! I am in despair.

(Enter Coligny with his entourage.)

GABRIEL

And here's Mr. Coligny who's come to confirm our disaster. Well, Lord Admiral, all is lost, even honor?

COLIGNY

No, friend, our defeat is more glorious than victory and the taking of our town is a triumph. Mr. de Guise has had time to arrive from Paris and troops from Piedmont; the towns, the men are prepared to defend the territory. The army can enter tomorrow on campaign. The realm is saved.

And all of this I can, I must say—all this thanks to you.

GABRIEL

Thanks to me?

COLIGNY

Eh, yes, thanks to you, you promised the King to make Saint Quentin resist eight days and made it resist twelve.

GABRIEL

Alas no, you are forgetting that in these last five days someone else—

COLIGNY

Well! But who was this someone else?

GABRIEL

Ah! Yes, who?

COLIGNY

Hey, your faithful and valiant squire.

GABRIEL

My squire.

COLIGNY

Why yes, the man right there! The enemy captains were complimenting him to me just now.

A demon of courage and audacity. Learning Saint Quentin was going to be taken before the date fixed, he rushed about, he multiplied himself, he rallied Beauregard, Lauxford, Captain Dumont, and urging on the leaders, inflamed the soldiers, armed the peasants with scythes, the children with stones, raising so to speak a hill before the foreigners, he did so well, so well harassed, disturbed, threatened the enemy, that he gave us— that he won—those five days for us.

GABRIEL

Martin Guerre!

MARTIN GUERRE

Ah, when I said I was a double. But that one, he's the real one, Milord, he's a good one.

GABRIEL

(embracing him) Ah! Yes, the good and the great! My brother! Why joy has cured me—and we have only one thing to do.

MARTIN GUERRE

Leave!

GABRIEL

Leave on the spot. Leave for Paris, for the Louvre.

COLIGNY

Impossible, Milord Vicomte! You are prisoner designate. You must wait until your ransom is gathered.

GABRIEL

Oh! Milord Admiral! It's because we must claim a promise from the King, a promise urgent and sacred.

(Diana de France enters.)

MARTIN GUERRE

Well! But as for me, I am not a prisoner. You will rejoin me as quickly as possible, Milord, but with your permission, I will go in advance, I will go to the King! Oh! You cannot refuse me, this honor!

GABRIEL

You call this honor, Martin Guerre, that signifies danger! There is still a danger and you still want to keep me away from it!

MARTIN GUERRE

For goodness sake!

GABRIEL

But in that case, reckon up the obstacles which will await you! They won't even consent to receive you! Who will open the royal gate for you?

DIANA de FRANCE

(coming forward) That will be me, I am leaving this morning for Paris with the Superior of the Benedictines, and if you like, Milord Vicomte, I shall have the honor of presenting the Squire Martin Guerre to the King.

CURTAIN

ACT III
SCENE 5

A room in the Louvre.

The Constable is alone

Diana de Poitiers enters, very agitated.

DIANA DE POITIERS

Are you quite happy? Don't you know what's happened?

CONSTABLE

Indeed! The king is with Mr. de Guise receiving our new army. As for me, I have found some share in our coffers, the money for my ransom, and today you were more beautiful than ever.

DIANA DE POITIERS

But do you know who's coming to us—who's coming to us from Saint Quentin?

CONSTABLE

Who? It cannot be Mr. d'Exmes, for the moment, thanks to the cunning of Mr. Arnold du Thil, he's a prisoner in Calais.

DIANA DE POITIERS

It's Diana de France and she insists on speaking right away.

CONSTABLE

Eh! Who cares! She cannot know anything. The one who might know something, the squire from hell, must have followed his master to Calais.

DIANA DE POITIERS

(seeing Arnould enter) Oh! Isn't that him?

ARNOULD

(enters, terrified) Milord. (stopping at the sight of Diana) Ah!

CONSTABLE

(laughing) Don't worry, Madame, it's precisely this Arnould de Thil—you are really quite bold, my comedian, to enter so abruptly.

ARNOULD

Ah! Milord! It's because I've just seen—

CONSTABLE

What is it? You'll excuse us, Madame? Go on! Speak and be brief—who did you see?

ARNOULD

Him—my look-alike.

CONSTABLE

Martin Guerre?

ARNOULD

In person.

CONSTABLE

(to Diana) Ah! Now this is more serious—where and when did you meet him?

ARNOULD

Here, in the courtyard of the Louvre, just now.

CONSTABLE

Did he see you?

ARNOULD

He saw me plainly.

CONSTABLE

Did he speak to you?

ARNOULD

With his eyes.

CONSTABLE

Frightened.

ARNOULD

Rather frightening.

CONSTABLE

You returned the audacity?

ARNOULD

By turning my back.

CONSTABLE

Coward! Afraid of your shadow.

ARNOULD

It's his fists I fear—

CONSTABLE

What do you know about them?

ARNOULD

I know myself, I'm very strong.

CONSTABLE

He pursued you?

ARNOULD

Like thunder.

CONSTABLE

Does he know he's got a twin?

ARNOULD

He must know.

CONSTABLE

Leave us, but don't go too far, perhaps I'll have to use you again.

ARNOULD

Very good! But now, Milord, the game is becoming devilishly risky.

CONSTABLE

Eh! Go, go will you?

(Exit Arnould de Thil.)

DIANA DE POITIERS

Well! Was I right to be fearful?

CONSTABLE

Yes, the Squire is coming in the place of, and in the name of, his master—and here's the danger confronting us.

DIANA DE POITIERS

Constable, it is terrible! If the prisoner—this Montgomery that I had the madness to love once—is given his liberty—he will deliver to the King—who's so jealous—proofs, letters which condemn me.

CONSTABLE

And you and I are ruined.

DIANA DE POITIERS

Ah, that will be your fault! Was it I, who, rather than bring about his death immediately let this wretch suffer for eighteen years? Is it I, who, instead of condemning him to death, condemned him to agony? O weakness disguised as pity! The rest of you men, you know indeed how to be cruel; why don't you have courage?

CONSTABLE

Diana!

DIANA DE POITIERS

Look! Now let's protect ourselves. We can still prevent this squire, a man of nothing from reaching the King.

CONSTABLE

On the contrary! It's better to do business with the unworthy son than the legitimate son.

DIANA DE POITIERS

Yes, but the King? The King is determined to keep his word.

(Fanfare outside.)

CONSTABLE

The King. Hold on, Diana, temptress of Kings—it's he returning. And it's on the King, I've told you that you can, that you must act.

DIANA DE POITIERS

O, the proposal that you advised me on is perhaps quite bold.

CONSTABLE

You are forgetting that the fairy Melusina was of your family of Poitiers, and I am going to repeat to you that you are more beautiful than ever.

(Enter the King.)

KING

You know that now, Madame, Diana, my daughter, the dear fugitive—we are going to see her.

DIANA DE POITIERS

Yes, Sire, and I'm rejoicing over it for you—more than you, perhaps.

KING

More then me?

DIANA DE POITIERS

The presence of your daughter may console you a bit over my absence when I am no longer near you.

KING

When you will no longer be near me?

DIANA DE POITIERS

Yes, Sire, I've just come to say goodbye. I'm leaving.

KING

What do you mean? What's going on?

CONSTABLE

Sire, the Squire of Mr. d'Exmes has just arrived from Saint Quentin.

KING

(shaking) Ah! He's arrived—the debt he's come to reclaim is serious, but, after all, it is a debt.

DIANA DE POITIERS

And yes, Your Majesty is determined, as is reasonable, to pay what he owes: he must.

CONSTABLE

And even to pay more than he owes. I remind the King already of the recent terms of the engagement he made in our presence.

DIANA DE POITIERS

Oh, but the King, my dear Constable, cannot keep to the precise letter of such a contract. That for you and for me his generosity may be severe, little matter! He agreed that the King would be merciful in doing justice. Only for me, I won't wait, with the return of the prisoner, the triumph of all who hate me at the court and Mr. de Montgomery, returning to the Louvre will drive me out.

CONSTABLE

He will drive us out, Madame.

KING

Eh, what! Both of you! You, my minister, you, my lady, you both would abandon me! No! It's impossible.

DIANA DE POITIERS

Sire, it's necessary. In an hour I'll have left Paris.

KING

Oh, but you are forgetting that my life is in you, I love you, Diana, I love you as on the first day—but you, do you no longer love me anymore?

DIANA DE POITIERS

Am I the one who refused to sacrifice the scruples of my conscience to my love? Oh! Yes, I love you, and a hundred times more than you love me! It's not the King I love, it's Henri, it's not Your Majesty, it's my chevalier. Ask the Constable what I was telling him just now. Ah, how I love you. All my joy and all my pride, it's to be your consort, not your mistress—not your serving girl! I don't see except through your eyes, I do not live, except through your soul. To leave—for me that would mean dying—(pause) I am leaving here in an hour—

KING

Diana! My Diana! (resisting) Ah! I cannot do otherwise than surrender this father to his sons.

DIANA DE POITIERS

Sire, I cannot do otherwise than submit myself to insult and to scorn.

KING

So, you will really leave? You will leave me alone? But what is it you want me to become without you? For so many years I've taken to only living for you! Look, see—on these walls on this furniture, everywhere, your monogram entwined with mine, like my life with yours. Your image under all forms fills my house and my heart. To efface your device from this dwelling, it would be necessary to destroy the Louvre, to efface your escutcheon from my heart would require tearing life from me.

DIANA DE POITIERS

I admire that you who are exiling me, reproach me for leaving—

KING

I am exiling you!

A PAGE (entering) Madame Diana de France asks the King permission to herself present to him a messenger from the Vicomte d'Exmes.

DIANA DE POITIERS

Oh! Could she know? I don't intend to blush before her. Goodbye.

KING

Listen.

DIANA DE POITIERS

Goodbye! (she leaves)

CONSTABLE

Sire, she's leaving!

KING

And I feel as if she were taking my life away. (to Page) We'll be with Madame Diane de France momentarily. (to Constable) Constable, come with me a bit to tell me again all that Mr. d'Exmes had promised.

(The King leaves with the Constable.)

(Martin Guerre and Madame Diane de France enter. They remain at the back near the door.)

MARTIN GUERRE

(agitated) Yes, Madame, yes, I saw this wretch who resembles me enter the Louvre, and I am certain he's the creature of the Constable and Madame de Poitiers.

DIANA de FRANCE

Eh! What can Madame de Poitiers and the Constable do?

MARTIN GUERRE

(in a half voice, as if to himself) What can a lion and a lioness do who are coming to tear apart their prey?

DIANA de FRANCE

We only have business with the King. Let me speak to him first. You see plainly that he had no difficulty receiving you. Be confident.

MARTIN GUERRE

Ah! If you know what it's all about.

DIANA de FRANCE

Will you be confident?

MARTIN GUERRE

Here it was many years ago, that I went forward, without doubting, patient and calm. But the obstacles on the route—battles, ambushes, assaults—they were nothing! The army of the enemy, that was nothing!

Today, near the goal, it seems to me that here I am before the true danger. So, I am actually glad that Gabriel was unable to come, and I am trembling he'll get here and my breast is heaving, my sight is troubled, I'm not exactly afraid, but I think I am worried.

DIANA de FRANCE

Worried! But for whom?

MARTIN GUERRE

Oh, not for me!

DIANA de FRANCE

The King! (pointing to the door at left)

Go in there.

MARTIN GUERRE

Oh! Madame, hasten, I'm waiting, I'm waiting.

(He leaves by the door at the left.)

KING

(entering with Diane de Poitiers) Yes, Diana, come receive with me my other Diana.

DIANA de FRANCE

(running to him) Sire.

KING

Ah, hug me, we've been really worried about you.

DIANA DE POITIERS

I am happy to see you, Madame.

KING

And overjoyed at the return of the prodigal child is much the greater because the prodigal child has filled her absence only with saintly and generous actions.

DIANA de FRANCE

The role of a woman is limited to small things but down there, I was witness to beautiful feats of arms and valiant actions.

KING

Speak of yourself; Mr. de Coligny will speak to me of others.

DIANA de FRANCE

Excuse me, Sire, I promised to speak to you about someone.

KING

Well, another day, you hardly got here.

DIANA de FRANCE

I promised to speak on my arrival. It's a question of the one who knew how to prolong the resistance of Saint Quentin for twelve days.

DIANA DE POITIERS

Oh—with the aid of my people and under the orders of the Admiral.

DIANA de FRANCE

Here's a letter from the Admiral, certifying in all honesty that without this blessed assistance, he would have been forced to surrender the town a dozen days sooner.

KING

Come on! So be it, in that case name the marvelous auxiliary.

DIANA de FRANCE

It's the Vicomte d'Exmes.

KING

Suffice, and when we see Mr. d'Exmes—again.

DIANA de FRANCE

He was taken prisoner to Calais, sire, and I engaged myself, after having been told the service rendered to remind you of the reward promised.

KING

(getting upset) The reward promised! Ah! He confided to you what the reward was. Well! Well, he swore the secret! He failed in his word; how dare he demand mine?

DIANA de FRANCE

I affirm to Your Majesty that, in apprising me what he had promised the King, he didn't even allow me catch a glimpse of what this reward might be. The gentleman kept his word and the King can keep his.

KING

(low to Diane de Poitiers) Oh! Madame what a cruel test!

DIANA de FRANCE

Whatever may be the reward that he is hoping for, he didn't tell me, Sire—but I know, but I've seen what superhuman will, what heroic effort, what passion and what fever the Vicomte d'Exmes has expended at every hour, at every minute, for twelve days.

Obstacles, dangers, exhaustion, injuries and death, nothing counted, nothing stopped him! He was terrifying, he was superb! Sire, I was present at these events and I understood. What this valiant man expected, what he wanted, it was something great and sacred which surpassed ambitions known in this world. And as for me, Sire, in your name, I repeated to him, this poor victorious prisoner, I confirmed to him that his King, that my father, would not be a bad debtor for this sublime debt.

KING

Well, my child, yes, surely I will acquit my debt. (to Diane de Poitiers) It seems, Madame, that Vicomte d'Exmes has revived the times of chivalry, by the feats that he has accomplished for the reward he had in view. I won't dicker with him over that reward.

DIANA DE POITIERS

(low to King) Henri, be careful!

DIANA de FRANCE

Ah, Sire, you are good! You are great!

KING

Wait then to praise me, flatterer! Mr. d'Exmes didn't tell you the reward he hopes from us, he ought not, he could not tell you. But now, my Diana, listen, he loves you, you love him, and despite the contrary plans of Madame and the Constable—the magnificent and charming reward he has earned, my daughter—and which I am giving him—well! It's you yourself.

DIANA de FRANCE

(aside) My God!

DIANA DE POITIERS

(aside) Ah! I breathe.

KING

Eh, what, you are quiet, Diana? You are not happy?

DIANA de FRANCE

Sire, I ask your pardon; what you are saying is not what you promised.

KING

What! How do you know? Then he did tell you?

DIANA de FRANCE

He told me nothing, but I know. At the hunting lodge in Saint Germain, when the Squire Martin Guerre gave the terrifying account, you made me go into the adjoining room, I heard everything. I know everything.

KING

Just Heaven!

DIANA de FRANCE

And now, father, I demand openly from you in the name of Mr. d'Exmes—freedom for his father.

(The King remains motionless.)

DIANA DE POITIERS

You are taking careful account, Diana, of what you are asking?

DIANA de FRANCE

Yes, truly, it's justice!

DIANA DE POITIERS

Justice cannot want the royal dignity to be compromised.

DIANA de FRANCE

What would compromise the royal dignity would be to betray an honest promise.

DIANA DE POITIERS

That would revive with the prisoner a mortal affront to the King.

DIANA de FRANCE

The grandeurs of pardon will cover the grandeurs of the offense.

DIANA DE POITIERS

You are leaguing against your father—with strangers you are forgetting filial piety.

DIANA de FRANCE

I'm not forgetting it, since I am protecting it.

DIANA DE POITIERS

By lacking it to your father?

DIANA de FRANCE

No, by believing his word.

DIANA DE POITIERS

You word, Henry? Then tell her what you just gave me in exchange for the love I keep for you.

DIANA de FRANCE

Father, you will prefer the promise that you undertook toward suffering!

KING

Ah! Silence, both of you! You are tearing my heart—one threatens me with her love, the other in her respect. Silence!

DIANA de FRANCE

But your decision?

KING

My decision, I don't owe to my daughter, I owe it to the son of the Count de Montgomery—and the son of the Count de Montgomery is absent.

DIANA de FRANCE

He's here, Sire, to await and receive that decision—another son of the count.

KING

Who is it? Ah! That Martin Guerre, the funereal witness! Well, so be it, let him come, I will reply to him, but to him alone. You, my daughter, leave me. You, too, yes, you yourself, Diana—may not be here. I desire that neither of you be here.

DIANA DE POITIERS

Sire, may God protect you.

(She leaves by the right.)

DIANA de FRANCE

I may seem to be pleading for the father of another, but it's you that I'm protecting, Father. It's for you yourself, that I entreat you again—I entreat you to have a soul and sleep in peace.

(She leaves by the back.)

(A Page enters.)

KING

Show in the envoy of Mr. d'Exmes. (the page leaves by the left. To himself) My God—which of the two of us has the most to fear from the other?

MARTIN GUERRE

(enters, bows) Sire.

KING

Come, I know all the great deeds that were done at Saint Quentin, I know what you are expecting of me.

MARTIN GUERRE

Ah, Sire, your first word is a word of encouragement. I was hoping for your kindness—I—I am listening, Majesty.

KING

(striding up and down with agitation) Yes, listen to me, listen to me to the end and understand me fully. Mr. d'Exmes deserves greatly of France and of us. If we followed only our inclination, we would grant him immediately what he asked. But Reason of State commands. We must consult, consider, we cannot risk diminishing in our person the royal power.

How you look at me, we cannot do it!

Does this mean we are tearing up the contract we agreed to? No! Only we are forced to reclaim the complete execution of it. So, Mr. d'Exmes has fulfilled only part of his undertaking.

Hey, where do you get that surprised look from?

You were there when your master settled the task upon himself.

"Sire," he said, "to purchase my father's freedom, I will hold the English eight days before Saint Quentin, and if that's not enough—and if that's not enough, I will retake the enemy one of the strongholds of which he is the master."

Were those his words, yes or no? Well—that's only half of what he said. He preserved Saint Quentin for twelve days—there's the city defended, but the city taken—where is it? Ham and Calais, Calais that key to France, are still, I believe, in the power of England.

Ah, you have no response to that! Nothing! The undertaking was bold? Is it more simple to set at liberty a criminal guilty of lese-majesty? To obtain the impossible, you offered the impossible; it wasn't done—! I still expect the unheard of service rendered to the state which will allow me to infringe on the laws of the State. You see, I am taking the trouble to explain all that to you. You are convinced, I think, and your master is going to be resigned to it.

Come on, answer now. Raise your eyes. Answer, what does this unsupportable silence mean?

MARTIN GUERRE

(motionless in a deep voice) How can I reply? Sire, you are the King; Sire, you have a hostage, with so dear and so fragile a life. While Your Majesty forbids me a word and a look—I was—in a dungeon. And I saw the old man who, for eighteen years, opened his eyes staring at the night. I saw the dying man that the executioner lies in wait for, and that an imprudent word from my mouth would finish. Oh! Sire! Allow me to be silent. Oh! My lips must allow nothing to escape all that roils in my heart—

Sire, be clement! I must not speak. I must not budge! I must not think.

KING

Then, you are only the mute messenger of Mr. d'Exmes.

MARTIN GUERRE

That's it! Let Your Highness merely deign to let me know exactly what I must say on your part to my master.

KING

Eh! But you know it.

MARTIN GUERRE

No, not exactly, Sire.

KING

(with effort) Well! You will tell Mr. d'Exmes that he has to fulfill to the end, his promise, and then, but only then, we will fulfill ours.

MARTIN GUERRE

Yes, I've completely understood; Mr. d'Exmes may obtain deliverance for his father only after having taken back from the enemy—Ham or Calais—that's all, Sire?

KING

That's all. Only it's doubtful, to say the truth, that he can undertake such an enterprise.

MARTIN GUERRE

Sire, what is it you want him to do? But there's yet one more thing—I still have in my mind a suspicion and a worry. While this son obstinately resumes his work, you remember, Sire? His father, the ghost with white hair—he could let a word escape and then he's to be cast into an airless dungeon which will kill him. You must judge—it's an idea, an image which must sometimes freeze this young man, who wakes with a start at night, and which gives him white hair. Must he still be told, Majesty, that the horrible law is in force? Will he have to think that his father may perhaps die while he's exposing his life to save him?

KING

(troubled) No—I will give orders; since the prisoner must live, his son will find him living.

MARTIN GUERRE

(breathing) Ah! Very fine! But may Your Majesty excuse me, I foresee a final question that Mr. d'Exmes is going to ask me. The undertaking by which he will attempt to reconquer a city seems to you impossible and senseless—?

KING

Hey, why risk it, this desperate act?

MARTIN GUERRE

Sire, we will risk it! We will risk it. But if this action fails, and his sons have perished, will the father not continue at least to wait and suffer—during days, nights, months, years, in the dark and forgetfulness? Will he then end his life without knowing that his sons have fought and died to free him?

KING

(moved) No! No! He will know it. He will have that consolation and that joy. He will be taken to some more distant prison where he will have light and air. You can tell that to Mr. d'Exmes, you can do it—bear my promise in your heart, my solemn promise.

MARTIN GUERRE

Well, this time, I am sure of it, Your Majesty will keep the promise especially if we do not not return to claim it from him.

(He bows deeply and goes to leave.)

KING

Stop! What is it you are saying? Is it necessary to remind me that you won't be coming back, wretch? And if you escape, if you succeed, do you imagine that I am going to tell you "that doesn't count?"

That you still must start over again? You think that? He thinks it! That's frightful what you are thinking, it's unworthy.

Well, no, no, it's fair—he's right and I deserve his scorn! Ah, it's no use for you to be silent, go on! I understand you. I've bargained and tricked your heroism, right! While you were playing with your lives, I was playing with words?

MARTIN GUERRE

(with shock) Oh! I didn't say that, Sire! I didn't say that!

KING

Hey, no. I'm the one, I'm the one saying it.

MARTIN GUERRE

Oh! Then, Sire, for the love of God, in that case free the prisoner as of now. You have seen the truth, humanity, justice! Give us our father, Sire! Ah, you can no longer not give him to us! Later, after we have Ham or Calais, don't worry, we will vanquish, we will kill as many as you like. But for pity, give us credit, give us this advance. Don't leave us longer in this anguish, in this distress frustrated of a boon that God alone can take back, orphans of a living father.

Free, free, Father!

KING

Ah, I'd like to do that, but I cannot. Diana! Diana! I too, am a prisoner. I have my hands tied and fatality has me in its grip.

MARTIN GUERRE

(with despair) Oh!

KING

But, look, is it so impossible that a city will be taken thanks to your brother? Mr. de Guise is his friend, and Mr. de Guise commands the army. Well, try, attempt, accomplish this new miracle and on my crown, on my soul! The Count de Montgomery will be set in liberty, instantly, and I double the wager—Mr. d'Exmes will marry Diana de France, my daughter and if I can help you in your attempt, call me! Ah! By my eternal salvation, I am with you this time against myself! Look, what is it that you say now? What is it you are thinking? Do you believe me at last? Do you still condemn me?

MARTIN GUERRE

Sire, I trust you! I trust you! It would be too horrible not to trust you! As for condemning you, or absolving you, let's both think of this prisoner—to each his torment. I have enough of mine—if you have yours, debate it with your conscience, it's a more powerful business than I am.

KING

That's fair! Goodbye, then and good luck! My daughter, ah! I don't want her to see me. Oh! Succeed! Succeed!

(He leaves hurriedly by the back.)

MARTIN GUERRE

(along to himself) He flees before his daughter because of my father.

DIANA de FRANCE

(entering) Martin Guerre!

MARTIN GUERRE

Oh! You are all atremble, Madame. What's wrong now?

DIANA de FRANCE

Mr. d'Exmes! Here is Mr. d'Exmes arrived from Calais.

MARTIN GUERRE

God!

DIANA de FRANCE

He's on my heels. I've seen him pale, feverish, half dead with anguish and fatigue. I went ahead of him to know? What has the King replied? I am "au courant" of all, and I've told Gabriel—what is the reply? Ah! There he is!

(Gabriel enters, breathless.)

MARTIN GUERRE

(aside) How to bring him this blow? (aloud, running to Gabriel) Eh! Quickly, get here, get here will you, Milord?

GABRIEL

Well—have you seen the King?

MARTIN GUERRE

Yes, good news! Good news! All is for the best.

GABRIEL

The King is going to return our father to us?

MARTIN GUERRE

Certainly! He's going to return him to us! He will return him to us!

GABRIEL

Right away?

DIANA de FRANCE

I was quite sure of it!

MARTIN GUERRE

Oh! But wait, wait a bit, a little patience, we had forgotten something, Milord—yes, a small supplementary debt.

GABRIEL

Oh—yet another delay!

DIANA de FRANCE

An obstacle!

MARTIN GUERRE

Eh, no, no—nothing I tell you—or at least a small thing. It's something admirable, it's that it's he, the scatterbrain, who promised it! The King reminded me of this word you gave, Gabriel, my word, as for me, I am touched in honor, I replied: without that, no deal.

GABRIEL

Oh, but what is it?

DIANA de FRANCE

What can the King demand?

MARTIN GUERRE

Ah! Know first of all, he is granting at the same time. The conditions fulfilled, my loverbirds, he will give you to each other.

GABRIEL

Diana! But still, what's it a question of?

MARTIN GUERRE

A question of? Well, My God, it's a question of taking Calais.

GABRIEL

Taking Calais?

MARTIN GUERRE

Eh, yes, Calais or another town. Since you promised a city, it must be delivered.

GABRIEL

Me, I promised? Ah! It's true! I remember, I remember now that shout, that bravado of my exalted filial love. Ah, today, the King insists—oh! That's abominable.

DIANA de FRANCE

Gabriel—pardon me!

MARTIN GUERRE

Gabriel! Come on! My child, be a man! Come on, no crying, no tears.

We don't have the time. Action! The King is forcing us. We must not complain of the King, Madame, we pity him. We were, perhaps, actually egoists to think only of our father; he's forcing us to free at the same opportunity, our mother, France—that's really fine.

We've never made a sulky face at danger nor at honor, right, Gabriel? It turns out you've just seen the fortifications of Calais—our friends, the Pequoy are in the place—Mr. de Guise is quite prepared with a wholly new army—ah! I laugh to think of it—fortune has fertilized for us, brother—let's go gaily to the harvest.

GABRIEL

Ah, with a companion such as you, discouragement is impossible. Let's go. Come! You, darling Diana, thanks and goodbye!

DIANA de FRANCE

Gabriel, you are returning to danger and perhaps death—and without me.

MARTIN GUERRE

Oh! Madame, it's really necessary that he win you!

When I tell you it's a magnificent campaign! It will be beautiful to return from it, hey—it would be beautiful to remain there!

CURTAIN

ACT IV
SCENE 6

The inside of a fisherman's hut. Nets and fishing apparatus hang from the wall. Doors left and right. Window at the back. Large chest leaning on the wall at back.

MACETTE

(alone, listening at an open window.) The musketry is silent on the Calais side.

(Enter Pillemiche, hesitating.)

MACETTE

Ah! Pillemiche, are you wounded dear friend?

PILLEMICHE

Yes and no, Macette of my heart. I passed back and forth through fire, without receiving, I believe, neither bruise nor wound, but I'm coming before the rest because my sword belt got torn and there's a barb which scratches me, but really scratches me.

MACETTE

Always fearless and delicate! (taking the belt) Give it to me—a thong that needs to be fixed, that's my concern. And has the day been good for the French?

PILLEMICHE

Yes and no, Macette darling. The English sortie was pushed back with losses, and we've picked up, not badly, some prisoners. But for the rest, we didn't quite get back into Calais with the enemy.

MACETTE

How you go on! In four days, Mr. de Guise has surprised the fort of Saint Agatha, carried the fort of Nieaully and Calais can no longer be reinforced by land.

PILLEMICHE

Yes, but on the sea side, there is that big wretched Fort Risbank.

MACETTE

Well, it only has to be taken too.

PILLEMICHE

By sea then? We lack a fleet, Macette. Our strongest warship would be, I really believe, Pape Anselme's fishing boat, the master of this shanty. In revenge, we saw just now an English ship set sail to go give the alarm at Dover and we are going to have a whole army under arms no later than tomorrow. That's why it would have been most useful to get into Calais today.

MACETTE

Why in that case, Mr. d'Exmes must be pretty worried?

PILLEMICHE

You could say despair, Macette.

MACETTE

And Mr. d'Exmes then, and Martin Guerre?

PILLEMICHE

Well, no! I don't know, as for them, they seem content, I've seen Martin Guerre rubbing his hands laughing.

MACETTE

Martin Guerre was laughing?

PILLEMICHE

He was laughing, yes, Macette. And yet I would have sworn that he wouldn't laugh until the day in which he'd caught and exterminated this Arnould du Thil—the author of his ills—and yours.

MACETTE

Pillemiche, as for me, I'll never laugh.

PILLEMICHE

Yes, Macette—you will smile and then you'll laugh and you will let this poor Pillemiche console you—after the real Martin Guerre has delivered you from the false.

MACETTE

Ah! When one thinks that this Arnould from the devil is still prowling in the neighborhood setting his snares under a dress quite like that of Martin Guerre.

PILLEMICHE

Yes, but Martin Guerre gives us every morning, a new password. And as for me, I who let myself be deceived too often by the imposter, I am sure of the ability to unmake him now—and if ever—(cocking an ear) Huh! What's that?

(The door opens on the left suddenly; Arnould du Thil rushes terrified into the room, but at the sight of Macette and Pillemiche, he crosses it in a few bounds and rushes out by the door at the right. Martin Guerre pursing him, enters from the left.)

MARTIN GUERRE

(running) Wait! Gallows bird! Good-for-nothing!

PILLEMICHE

Arnould du Thil!

MACETTE

We're going to get him.

(Pillemiche and Macette rush out to the right. Arnould du Thil puts a leg over the ledge of the window and comes back, crouching, into the room.)

MARTIN GUERRE

Alert! A spy! (outside left)

PILLEMICHE

(outside right) Over this way!

(Arnould du Thil runs back and forth, undecided, he spies the trunk at the back, opens it and crouches inside letting the cover fall back.)

MARTIN GUERRE

(in the doorway at the left) Where is he, the scoundrel?

PILLEMICHE

(reentering, by the right, seizing Martin Guerre by the throat) I've got you, bandit!

MACETTE

(in the door on the right) Don't release him, the monster!

MARTIN GUERRE

Hey, it's me, Martin Guerre.

PILLEMICHE

Tell that to someone else.

MARTIN GUERRE

But it's me! Me! Me!

PILLEMICHE

Then the password—who do you see in the mirror.

MARTIN GUERRE

The image that can't be seen.

PILLEMICHE

Oh, pardon, good Martin Guerre! I really thought to have nabbed Arnould du Thil!

MARTIN GUERRE

(rubbing his neck) And even one idea more, you were strangling him.

(shaking his hand) Thanks! Oh, the two of us cannot remain on the same Earth! And he's escaped me again.

PILLEMICHE

And from me!

MACETTE

Yes, you have no luck, for once you got him—and it's not him!

MARTIN GUERRE

(sitting on the chest) What! That spy! That robber, that traitor who's already done us so much harm—and who can yet ruin our dear hope, I won't stop until I've succeeded in lynching the rogue a little.

PILLEMICHE

Oh! I've given the word to our posts and our patrols—if he wanders into the woods at night, they'll catch him and bring him to us—ah—here are our folks with some prisoners.

(Malemort and six or seven mercenaries bringing in prisoners, among them Jean Peuquoy and Jack Tobin.)

MALEMORT

Master, our prisoners—what's to be done with 'em?

MARTIN GUERRE

Here's what's to be done. (hugs Jean) Hello, Cousin.

JEAN

Cousin, hello.

ALL THE MERCENARIES

Huh? What's going on?

MARTIN GUERRE

Eh, no, these enemies are friends. We didn't capture them, they got captured. Ah, my good comrades, recruited and chosen amongst the veterans of the wars of Lorraine and Italy, you and your companions are the elite of the fourteen brave men who will follow, I believe, our leader, Mr. d'Exmes to hell. Well, these good Calaises, these good Frenchmen are worthy of fighting beside you. I've told you that tonight we have a great blow to strike—here are those who will help us do it.

JEAN

Still, I ask that they guard strongly chained and watched over our dear Lieutenant Jack Tobin, who didn't let himself be captured but who actually was duly captured.

JACK TOBIN

Oh, as for me! Jacques Tobin, in name, in heart, in accent, French.

JEAN

Oh, you are French and you know how to pronounce French when the French are victorious.

JACK TOBIN

(low to Martin Guerre) Mr. Martin Guerre—help me—you recognize me.

MARTIN GUERRE

Eh! This is the first time I've seen you, my dear fellow.

JACK TOBIN

Oh—you are forgetting Saint Quentin and our good little traffic with Your Master and your relative.

MARTIN GUERRE

What! Wretch! It's you who sold them! And you are taking me for Arnould du Thil, my frightful double.

JACK TOBIN

I've heard talk—that resemblance but then I also detest Arnould du Thil. He corrupted me.

MARTIN GUERRE

Come on, enough! My friends, we have to discuss things, Jean and me. Go in there, Macette, serve them your best wine. In three minutes we will bring you the plan for the feast.

JACK TOBIN

Mr. Martin Guerre, I scorn Arnould du Thil.

MARTIN GUERRE

Go! Take away this amphibian.

(Pillemiche drags off Tobin, all leave by the right.)

MARTIN GUERRE

And now, cousin, to our fame. Ah—this is the great role.

(Jean goes to listen at the door on the left. Martin Guerre to himself)

MARTIN GUERRE

Supreme role, My God! Which can at last deliver father. Meanwhile, let's try not to expose our brother too much. (aloud) First, Jean, let's agree carefully on our acts and facts.

JEAN

(at the door) Aren't we going to wait for Pierre Peuquoy? (he comes back)

MARTIN GUERRE

Pierre? At this moment, Mr. d'Exmes is presenting him to the Duke De Guise to calm that dear general a bit. Ah! Because he wasn't very young or very tender just now. He said to us—Holy God! You've dreamed the impossible! Tomorrow can you make the flag of France replace the flag of England flying over Fort Risbank when the English vessels arrive from Dover to see it? Look, can you do it?

JEAN

In that case, Pierre is in the process of explaining to him how we were left, we bourgeois, to guard this Fort Risbank that they judge inaccessible to the French.

But if we can introduce there a company of Frenchman, however small it may be, that of Mr. d'Exmes, for example, we will convince the irresolute and terrify the fearful—and the impossible will become almost possible.

MARTIN GUERRE

Completely possible, cousin.

JEAN

Yes, save some slim danger of death.

MARTIN GUERRE

Oh, so small a thing! Still, you know, Jean, that in face of danger—I always leave the largest share to Mr. d'Exmes—the lion's share.

JEAN

Ah! You leave it to him?

MARTIN GUERRE

So, after our plan, tonight we are alleged to divide into two our small troupe—to be separately commanded, by Gabriel and myself—and consequently, to go, each by our side.

JEAN

Yes—there'll be an expedition on land and on sea.

MARTIN GUERRE

Well, between ourselves, cousin, which be the more perilous, eh? The most worthy of them, Milord?

JEAN

(laughing) Oh, that jumps right out at you, Martin Guerre!

MARTIN GUERRE

Yes, evidently, the serious danger will be for those who try to enter by land with you in Calais.

JEAN

No, indeed, no, indeed! Those inside expect us, in our turn, to bring them prisoners; we lead them quite calmly to Fort Risbank, we unchain them quite gently at the appointed hour and give them their arms in friendship.

MARTIN GUERRE

Yes, but then the better half of the bourgeois militia declares themselves for England, a terrible battle ensures—come on—I won't hesitate to reserve for Milord, this glorious adventure.

JEAN

Ah, indeed! Do you want to make me believe it—it's the stroke from the sea which will run the real danger?

MARTIN GUERRE

The blow from the sea? It's amusing and that's all.

JEAN

Amusing! To put eight men in a fishing boat from Anselme's to confront at night the reefs of Fort Risbank.

MARTIN GUERRE

A stroll under the stars—

JEAN

To clamber up the rocks with hands, feet, fingernails, to scale under fire, and with the aid of a simple rope ladder a vertical wall of 180 feet.

MARTIN GUERRE

A climb in fine air!

JEAN

With no possibility of turning back because the boat cannot be moored and the sea will engulf the coward or he who is imprudent enough to attempt to retreat back down.

MARTIN GUERRE

Well, but since we intend to climb!

JEAN

Yes, but at the summit, one very much risks being received by the lances and blunderbusses of the English and finding oneself suspended by a hemp knot between death from above and the abyss below.

MARTIN GUERRE

Exciting situation! And decidedly the sea, death by drowning, the ascent, the squall, the battle all these details tempt me. Bah, let Milord take the danger for himself, as for me, I keep that pleasure for myself.

JEAN

Yeah! From selfishness, right?

MARTIN GUERRE

My word, yes, each for himself, the one of climbers who run the greatest risk—that will be certainly for the last.

JEAN

Damn! The least false step of all the others will precipitate him. and still to serve as the person bringing up the rear—to the soldiers, it's necessary that the last be the chief.

MARTIN GUERRE

And that would be Gabriel! No! No! (aloud) So much the worse for Mr. d'Exmes—that will be me! That will be me!

JEAN

Yes, yes, intriguing! You intend as usual to take the blows on yourself and leave the honor to him.

MARTIN GUERRE

What do you mean? (aside) Why is it as plain as that? The Devil! Let's pay attention.

(Gabriel and Pierre Peuquoy enter.)

MARTIN GUERRE

Well! Mr. de Guise?

PIERRE

Mr. de Guise is a great man.

GABRIEL

If, at day break, we have hoisted the French flag over Fort Risbank, he will support us with a decisive assault.

PIERRE

So long as I don't die between now and then!

GABRIEL

Where are our people?

MARTIN GUERRE

There.

GABRIEL

We must put them "au courant" quickly.

JEAN

Hold on! Jack Tobin is with them.

MARTIN GUERRE

Hey! Are we leaving him in the camp?

JEAN

No—it's better that he reenter Calais with us.

PIERRE

Luck is turning on our side; Tobin will bring over the suspicious precisely because he is suspicious.

JEAN

Still—it would be wise to keep him unaware of the great plan.

MARTIN GUERRE

That's easy. (he calls) Master Jack Tobin.

JEAN

(entering) Here! (noticing Pierre, who gives a military salute) Oh, my Captain.

MARTIN GUERRE

Master Tobin, we have something to say to the brave men who are in there. You're not one of them. Wait for us here.

JEAN

And don't budge. You are in the midst of the French camp.

(Martin Guerre, Gabriel, and Peuquoy leave by the right. Arnould du Thil raises the lid of the trunk.)

JACK TOBIN

(turning towards the door at the right) If you please, Mr. Martin Guerre, I detest Arnould du Thil the way you do.

ARNOULD

(emerging from the trunk, aside) Ah! You want to lynch me—ah—the two of us cannot remain on the same earth.

JACK TOBIN

(still talking at the door) Martin Guerre, you will see if Arnould du Thil falls under my hand again—I—(he makes a gesture of massacre, Arnould du Thil lays his hand on his shoulder) Oh—

Martin Guerre, again!

ARNOULD

Arnould du Thil—silence! (showing him a purse) Twenty gold crowns for you—you'll get more later.

JACK TOBIN

Oh! What must I do in advance?

ARNOULD

Tonight you will be with Pierre and Jean Peuquoy on the platform of Fort Risbank, the French will scale the big tower by means of a rope ladder.

JACK TOBIN

Oh!

ARNOULD

You will let them all peacefully pass—but the last one before he's placed his foot or his knee on the parapet—you'll hurl yourself on him, and you'll precipitate him from the height of the tower.

JACK TOBIN

Oh! But the others will be in a fury against me.

ARNOULD

No! You will say, "It was that scalawag Arnould du Thil—he fell under my hand." (he repeats the gesture Tobin just made)

JACK TOBIN

I don't understand very well.

ARNOULD

You have no need to understand. No danger for you and twenty gold crowns. (he gives him the purse)

JACK TOBIN

Oh! I understand this purse.

ARNOULD

And you are determined to make the little push.

JACK TOBIN

Well—yes!

(Noise in the room at the right.)

ARNOULD

They are coming back—the last one, make no mistake! The last one.

JACK TOBIN

The last one.

(Arnould leaves running by the left.)

JEAN

(enters, giving Tobin a sword and a dagger) Here, Jack Tobin, I'm returning your arms to you—rejoin there our bourgeois who are returning to Calais.

JACK TOBIN

Oh! But who then is victorious?

JEAN

The French! The French! The French!

(Jack Tobin leaves by the right. Martin Guerre, Gabriel, and Pierre enter.)

MARTIN GUERRE

My friends, consider, once again, you are completely overturning the plan I arranged so well.

GABRIEL

It has to be. It must be me who heads the scaling of Fort Risbank.

JEAN

And you, Martin Guerre, you will command those of your men that we are supposed to bring as prisoners into Calais.

PIERRE

Come on! Give up your sword and let's march.

MARTIN GUERRE

My first place is then really so impossible?

GABRIEL

Eh! Yes, impossible! We just proved it to you.

JEAN

No question; since we are obliged to pass before Lord Grey, the Governor of Calais.

PILLEMICHE

He doesn't know you, Martin Guerre; but he will recognize Mr. d'Exmes, his former prisoner.

GABRIEL

He'd detain me, and all would be compromised.

MARTIN GUERRE

Ah! An idea—if the two of us, Milord and myself, stayed for the scaling—

JEAN

No—we must have a leader your men will obey.

MARTIN GUERRE

Oh! My God!

PILLEMICHE

Mr. d'Exmes, take this horn for the signal. I'm the one who made it, and I'll answer for it as he—(pointing to Jean)—answered for his rope ladder—we will hear it even in the storm, come on—let's be off—en route!

MARTIN GUERRE

Ah! My dear Lord, is it really necessary that you climb up last?

JEAN

From the moment it's a question of Mr. d'Exmes, it's no longer a pleasure?

PILLEMICHE

Mr. d'Exmes still doesn't seem to be sulking.

GABRIEL

Do you know, friend, you will end by offending me.

MARTIN GUERRE

Be quiet—your father's watching you; you also have the right to expose yourself for him! (he hugs him) I confide you to God! (he leaves by the left with Pierre and Jean Peuquoy)

(Night has fallen—the hovel is dark.)

GABRIEL

(watching Martin Guerre leave) He is capable of coming back! Oh, let's hurry. I want to have an enterprise and a danger for myself alone. (he goes to open the door at right) Come, come quickly my brave companions.

(The mercenaries enter.)

GABRIEL

All is clearly understood and explained, right? When your ship, Anselme, touches the rock of Fort Risbank, I will sound the horn. Pierre Peuquoy will answer us from the height of the tower—Jean Peuquoy will toss us his rope ladder—the most exposed in the scaling will be the one who climbs last—I will be that one.

PILLEMICHE

I thought it would be Martin Guerre.

GABRIEL

No, no! It will be me—what's that noise?

PILLEMICHE

(going to the door at the left) A patrol is bringing us a man.

MALEMOST

Eh! It's Martin Guerre!

GABRIEL

(enraged) Ah! I was sure of it!

(Four men present themselves, in the middle Arnould du Thil.)

PILLEMICHE

One moment, the password—what do you see in the mirror?

ARNOULD

The image that can't be seen.

(Pillemiche gestures to the patrol, who release Arnould and leave.)

PILLEMICHE

Ah! Martin Guerre, I knew indeed that you would get here—to be the last to climb.

ARNOULD

(aside, with shock) The last! I'm a dead man!

GABRIEL

Well, no, no Martin Guerre! I will not cede this last danger to you. I will climb only after you—this time, I intend—I am taking the honor for myself.

ARNOULD

(aside) Good! And death!

GABRIEL

(to Mercenaries) Arrange yourselves in the order of the escalate—Pillemiche, you will climb first.

PILLEMICHE

Thanks, Milord.

GABRIEL

Then Malemost, Anselme, Lactance, the two Sharfensteins, finally Martin Guerre and me.

(He arranges them.)

ARNOULD

(aside) And meanwhile, as I rid myself of my enemy, Jack Tobin's going to rid the Constable of his.

GABRIEL

We will rest only at the 100th echelon, and only for time to count to sixty. I have no need to remind intrepid men such as yourselves that once adventuring on the ladder no retreat is possible. The Gulf will pardon the coward who tries to come back down even less than the enemy.

ARNOULD

(aside) Diavolo! We must climb.

GABRIEL

And now—forward under God's protection.

ALL

Forward!

(They leave by the left in the order indicated.)

CURTAIN

ACT IV
SCENE 7

The side of the ocean at Calais. To the right and the back, the sea and some crests of rocks protruding from the sea. To the left, the massive walls forming part of the central tower of Risbank, whose base is lost in the bottom and whose summit it lost in the fog. It's night. Through the noise of the wave and wind one hears resonate from below the first call of the horn, then a second. A rope ladder descends and uncoils down the side of the tower, then seems to settle and extend to its lower extremity.

At the end of a few seconds, a head appears visible on the last steps, it's Pillemiche climbing up, followed by Malemost and the other companions.

They silently rise up the length of the tower, which has the appearance of slowly lowering itself. Pillemiche stops and then, for a moment those who follow him remain motionless.

Malemort (touching Pillemiche's leg) Go forward, will you?

PILLEMICHE

I cannot anymore.

MALEMORT

Why?

PILLEMICHE

I have vertigo.

MACETTE

(leaning towards the third) The first has vertigo.

(One hears repeated "the first has vertigo.)

MACETTE

Here's Mr. d'Exmes climbing up.

(Clinging to the rope, he places his food by that of Malemost.)

GABRIEL

(to Pillemiche) Do you intend to advance?

PILLEMICHE

I have vertigo.

GABRIEL

Will you advance.

PILLEMICHE

I will fall and I will make you all fall.

GABRIEL

(placing his dagger between Pillemiche's shoulders) Do you feel the point of my dagger?

PILLEMICHE

Ah! Mercy.

GABRIEL

If you don't go forward, I'll kill you.

PILLEMICHE

(terrified) Oh! Pardon! I obey!

GABRIEL

Ah! Martin Guerre has got what he wished; he's the last.

(The horn sounds and the noise of distant battle in the town. Gabriel, who has taken the place of Malemost, climbs after Pillemiche, followed by the others. After a few moments, their ascension leads the platform of the tower. In the space that the tower hides, appears, extending in a half circle, the square of Calais with its forts, its ramparts and its loopholes from which shine distant lights. Pierre Peuquoy, Jean Peuquoy, and the Bourgeois of the Militia receive the arrivals and help them cross the parapet.)

JACK TOBIN

(aside) I'm waiting for the last. (after the sixth, he leans over the parapet) Hey, climb up will you last one or I'll cut the ladder. (the head of Arnould du Thil appears. Tobin rushes at him)

ARNOULD

It's me, Arnould, I—(but Tobin cannot arrest his movement and Arnould, pushed, falls, uttering a terrible scream)

GABRIEL

(to Tobin) Wretch! What have you done?

JACK TOBIN

Hey, I killed Arnould du Thil.

MARTIN GUERRE

(coming forward) Not at all, Praise God, Milord, it actually was Arnould du Thil.

GABRIEL

Oh! Your blood is shed. (throwing himself in his arms)

MARTIN GUERRE

Yes, for you I always have luck.

(The early light of day illuminates the horizon. A cannon shot echoes in the distance.)

MARTIN GUERRE

Mr. de Guise is waking up. Fort Risbank is ours and in two hours, Calais belongs to France. Long live France!

ALL

Long live France!

CURTAIN

ACT V
SCENE 8

At Tournelles. The King's tent allowing to be seen at the back, when it is open, the battlefield, the barriers and the stand.

CONSTABLE

(to a herald) The King, when he comes to rest here will designate a queen of the tournament for the second joust, the judge of the camp and the contenders who will break their lances against him.

(the herald leaves)

DIANA DE POITIERS

(who's just entered) Ordinarily, for this second half of the day, the Constable was the judge designated and Diane de Poitiers was queen by right. Why's the custom change today? Why hasn't the King even addressed a word to me?

CONSTABLE

Diana, since yesterday he seems to be avoiding me also.

DIANA DE POITIERS

What! Could it be caused by the first news received from Calais? Was the news so favorable?

CONSTABLE

Two forts were surprised and carried by the avant-guard, nothing more—and yet—

DIANA DE POITIERS

Finish. Do you actually think that our adventurous adversaries could have had this unheard of success?

CONSTABLE

Well, yes, Diana! I told you, trembling, they are capable, these madmen, the other great madman—Mr. de Guise, assisting, they are capable of taking Calais.

DIANA DE POITIERS

Ah—then there will be no more resources.

CONSTABLE

The King, without wishing to hear anything, will deliver Montgomery.

DIANA DE POITIERS

Oh! But then, are we going to wait for him to be freed?

CONSTABLE

What? What is your thought?

DIANA DE POITIERS

My Friend! If the King dies—we will be, you and I, the same day—driven from the Louvre, exiled from Paris—Well! say to yourself that the same fate threatens us without the shortest delay, if the prisoner doesn't die in secret—

CONSTABLE

(looking at her.) But—for him to die—he must speak.

DIANA DE POITIERS

Is it impossible that he will speak—this man condemned to silence?

CONSTABLE

Oh—if they went to him at this moment and whispered to him—your son's going to come! Your son's going to deliver you—no question he would let a word, a name, a shout escape.

DIANA DE POITIERS

And we would be saved!

CONSTABLE

Diana! Oh! That would be frightful!

DIANA DE POITIERS

But we would be saved. No, that's not what I ought to say to devotion such as yours, "my friend, I will be saved!"

CONSTABLE

The King—well, Diana, well! I'm going to attempt to save you. (he leaves by the left)

(The King enters all in armor except for his helmet—he gives his arm to Diana de France—along with ladies, gentleman, pages—etc.)

DIANA de FRANCE

Sire, you are in truth the most brilliant knight in your realm. And when you are seen in the lists—one understands why you adore this noble sport of tournament.

KING

Today, Diana, I feel, to tell the truth, in the mood of victory. Also, we have the pleasure, my dear daughter, to name you queen of the second joust.

DIANA DE POITIERS

(aside) She! Diana de France!

KING

Milord Admiral will be the judge of the camp. (enter Coligny, all upset, noises off) Eh! But what's going on, Milord Admiral? What's happening?

COLIGNY

Sire, pardon, there are some good folks who wish to speak to Your Majesty. The King will excuse them if they are a little dusty and embarrassed by a journey of seventy leagues.

(Enter hurriedly Pierre and Jean Peuquoy, three or four bourgeois, Martin Guerre, Gabriel.)

KING

Ah—come close, my friends.

PIERRE and JEAN

The King.

PIERRE

(troubled—to Jean) Well—the thing—you have it—give it then.

JEAN

(to Pierre—delivering the keys) But the disk—you have the disk.

KING

Oh—speak! Speak quickly!

(Pierre, knee on the ground, presents the keys on a vermillion platter.)

PIERRE

Sire, the keys—Sire—the emotion—Sire, I am French—good

French.

KING

Yes, and so good French, friend, French so deeply moved that one understands nothing of your harangue. Come on, help him, you—Martin Guerre.

MARTIN GUERRE

Me, Sire? Well, the keys that Pierre Peuquoy is offering and presenting to Your Majesty are the keys of your good city of Calais.

KING

Of Calais?

MARTIN GUERRE

Yes, Calais—retaken in four hours and French—now and forever!

KING

Ah—then we can revive today the old shout of former passes at arms

Praise God! Joy to France!

ALL

Joy to France!

KING

And now, Martin Guerre, name us the one who was the arm of this marvelous enterprise.

MARTIN GUERRE

The two good and robust arms of the enterprise—here they are, Sire—it's Pierre Peuquoy, the armorer, and Jean Peuquoy, the weaver.

KING

Why then, who was at the head?

MARTIN GUERRE

Sire, it's our great and illustrious Captain the Duke, François de Guise.

KING

But finally tell, will you, who conceived the plan, forces the means, realized the idea?

MARTIN GUERRE

(pointing to Gabriel) That one, he's there—It's up to Your Majesty to name him.

ALL

The Vicomte d'Exmes.

KING

Not at all the Vicomte d'Exmes, the Vicomte de Montgomery.

(Sounds of astonishment.)

KING

Yes, gentleman! The Vicomte de Montgomery; which means the Count de Montgomery is still living. (to Gabriel) To redeem and deliver your father, sir, you've accepted, you've accomplished two heroic conditions, and you've twice over earned your sublime reward.

GABRIEL

Oh! Sire!

KING

Don't be afraid, if for a new reward I propose a new condition that won't be difficult to fulfill—it's to touch our escutcheon and to break with us one last lance today.

GABRIEL

Such an honor.

KING

Oh—you are going to justify it. God fights so visibly with you that you can be certain in advance of victory.

MARTIN GUERRE

Not against you, Sire.

KING

Especially against me. (to Diana de France) Queen of the tourney, you yourself will deliver the prize to the victor.

DIANA de FRANCE

Sire, there are actually changes for the ring to come back to Your Majesty.

KING

(taking Diana's hands to his lips) Don't worry, pretty one! We will reserve in that case to our adversary a more previous gift.

DIANA de FRANCE

My generous father.

GABRIEL

Majesty.

KING

This time, sir, I intend to go beyond my promises—I intend that you be satisfied—to be satisfied myself—and no, go, go—arm yourself quickly.

(Gabriel bows and leaves.)

KING

My horse—Martin Guerre! Well, friend—so you don't wish under any shape to accept your role?

MARTIN GUERRE

My role? Ah! Sire, you know what I am waiting for—it's as fine and beautiful as any sovereign in this world can give.

KING

And when you have it, do you think I will be quiet?

MARTIN GUERRE

Yes, I think so.

KING

But the prisoner, will he speak like you?

MARTIN GUERRE

Sire, I hope it.

KING

(pensive) Stay then, God! Come on! Friend, come, come with me. I'm in a rush to acquit myself and you are going to see that I am ready. (he goes towards the lists with Martin Guerre, Diana de France and all others present except Diane de Poitiers, leave with them)

DIANA DE POITIERS

(to herself) Not a word, not one look for me! Ah, we are indeed, truly lost, if the Constable—

(The Constable enters from the left.)

CONSTABLE

All must be done.

DIANA DE POITIERS

You've seen the prisoner?

CONSTABLE

I've seen the governor of the prisoner.

DIANA DE POITIERS

But the prisoner?

CONSTABLE

I gave orders.

DIANA DE POITIERS

The prisoner? The prisoner?

CONSTABLE

They must have gone into his cell.

DIANA DE POITIERS

(with a scream of rage) Ah—you didn't go down yourself?

CONSTABLE

Diana, I didn't dare!

DIANA DE POITIERS

Come on! I will still have all the adversity alone—Come! I am going straight to the King.

(She heads toward the gate at the right. Martin Guerre appearing in the gateway.)

MARTIN GUERRE

Pardon—Madame. I'm ordered to guard this entry.

CONSTABLE

Who dares to bar the way to Madame Diane de Poitiers?

MARTIN GUERRE

Eh! Why, first of all, the King, I believe.

DIANA DE POITIERS

It's the King I intend to speak—

MARTIN GUERRE

Yes, to seduce him again into perjury. But beware—the King, thank God, doesn't even wish to hear you.

DIANA DE POITIERS

Let me beware, me! Sometimes people have been afraid of Diane de Poitiers but Diane de Poitiers is rarely afraid. Ah, you rely on the King, blind man that you are—and you are forgetting that the King loves me! He's loved me for many years, he'll love me until his last breath. Truly, I pity the fool who will dare to oppose me so long as Henry II is living, while his heart beats—which only beats for me.

MARTIN GUERRE

Oh—you mistake me, Madame, it's not on the King we are relying. The King—why all we have done, was done without him—and despite him. And yet you actually imagine that we didn't do it alone.

Think of this and speak less loudly I invite you. I find you sovereignly imprudent—to want to argue with punishment. Day of God! When you see the light shine you ought to look at it twice before provoking the lightening.

DIANA DE POITIERS

Make way! I don't know what it is to recoil before these phantoms.

MARTIN GUERRE

That's because you've never seen them.

(Montgomery appears in the doorway at the right, beard and hair, white—pale, round-shouldered, wrapped in a long black velour cloak. Martin Guerre runs to him and supports him.)

DIANA DE POITIERS and the CONSTABLE

(recoiling, terrified) God!

MARTIN GUERRE

Oh, don't worry. My Lord is not coming to see his executioners. Only keep back so he can see his son. (the large curtain at the back opens—the lists appear—the trumpet sounds) And your son, Milord, hold on—there he is breaking a lance against the King—and all the more proud and happy knowing that his father's watching him.

(Fanfare, the King and Gabriel armed for a tournament present their horses prancing. At the first meeting they salute with their lances. At the second, they both break them.)

MARTIN GUERRE

Two lances broken! Even joust.

(Another fanfare. This time Gabriel hits the King's helmet with his truncheon—the King's helmet breaks. The King lets out a scream and falls backward on the rump of his horse.)

CONSTABLE

Ah! The King struck in the face—knocked over, wounded.

DIANA DE POITIERS

God, if the King's dead, his death's going to kill me.

(The King is surrounded by the dazed crowd and all those present. They bring the King in on a stretcher.)

DIANA de FRANCE

Father—My God—is he actually dead?

KING

(pulling himself up) Mr. de Montgomery, are you there? (all give way before Montgomery, who, leaning on Martin Guerre, marches to the King)

KING

Count, I am going to die, do you pardon me?

MONTGOMERY

Sire, I am going to die, let us pardon each other.

KING

My daughter, your hand—Gabriel. (he places the hand of Diana into that of the despairing Gabriel) Don't be desolate; it was not you who struck—I recognize you, sovereign justice—(he dies)

MARTIN GUERRE

Receive him, clement sovereign.

CURTAIN

(NOTE—there is a special simplified version for the provinces that do not have the two actors who look enough alike to play Martin Guerre and Arnould du Thil. This version allows for one actor to play both parts. Also the scenes can be simplified.)

ABOUT THE AUTHOR

Frank J. Morlock has written and translated many plays since retiring from the legal profession in 1992. His translations have also appeared on Project Gutenberg, the Alexandre Dumas Père web page, Literature in the Age of Napoléon, Infinite Artistries.com, and Munsey's (formerly Blackmask). In 2006 he received an award from the North American Jules Verne Society for his translations of Verne's plays. He lives and works in México.

www.ingramcontent.com/pod-product-compliance
Lightning Source LLC
LaVergne TN
LVHW041618070426
835507LV00008B/314